Daniel

ENGLAND'S HEROES

2018

ENGLAND'S HEROES
2018

A TRIBUTE TO OUR YOUNG LIONS

HarperCollins*Publishers*

CONTENTS

FOREWORD

This was the summer when England fell in love with their national team again – creating dreams of glory that will last for decades. Across the country, children are emulating their heroes, playing at being Harry Kane, Kieran Trippier or Jordan Pickford. For the first time in a generation, kids believe that England can be champions, and that will fire them up to become internationals themselves.

Fans old enough to remember Italia 90 – the last time the Three Lions reached a World Cup semi-final – will never forget how proud we felt to see England up there with the best on the global stage. We aren't used to it – even those who were around for the heroics of 1966.

In 2018, as the nation basked in a heatwave, Gareth Southgate's England gave us hope again. The World Cup in Russia had (almost) everything:

A young, inexperienced Three Lions side, many from humble beginnings.

A nail-biting victory in the first game.

A record-breaking six-goal rout as fans enjoyed a Sunday in the sunshine.

A hat-trick by an Englishman.

Our first victory in a World Cup penalty shoot-out. YES, WE WON ON PENALTIES!

Germany dumped out in the group stage.

Argentina, Spain, Portugal and even five-time winners Brazil all going home before us.

And our captain winning the Golden Boot.

Everywhere you went, people were happy, parties were going on, neighbours would come round to watch the game. Even non-football fans got swept up in World Cup fever. Crowds gathered to share every moment on giant screens, like this lot in London's Hyde Park, pictured. We were all as one, kicking every ball, going through the agony and the ecstasy together.

Modest manager Southgate, who should take so much credit for the young lions' success in Russia, didn't want any fuss when the squad came home, so this book is *The Sun*'s tribute to him and all 23 members of a smart, close-knit and likeable England squad who should hold their heads high, having made 2018 the best summer we could have asked for.

Football didn't come home this time. But now we know that one day, it will.

SOUTHGATE: ERA OF THE WAISTCOAT

He was the FA 'Yes man' who had consistently said 'No' to the FA. He was the nice guy who kept making ruthless decisions. He was the bloke who missed a decisive spot-kick and then discovered the way to win a penalty shoot-out for England.

Gareth Southgate was an underwhelming choice as Three Lions' manager – and yet, in the glorious steaming-hot summer of 2018, he ended up overwhelming all England. Southgate had stepped up from his role as Under-21s boss to take temporary charge following Sam Allardyce's departure on 27 September 2016, just one game into his reign.

After presiding over two wins and two draws, Southgate signed a four-year deal on 30 November to become England's fourth permanent manager in as many years. And so began the Three Lions' unlikely journey to World Cup dreamland. No previous England boss with as much tournament experience as Southgate had taken the job – he went to two European Championships and two World Cups as a player, then coached his nation's Under-21 side at several summer showpieces. And after the glories of the 2018 World Cup campaign came the realisation that this underestimated man, with his strong convictions and quiet intelligence, had learned well from that wealth of experience.

Southgate was born in Watford and raised in Crawley, where his youth football team would train in a multi-storey car park due to a lack of facilities. But he is now an adopted Yorkshireman, having lived in an impressive six-bedroom, 16th-century manor house near Harrogate for the past dozen years. There, he and Alison, his wife of 21 years, have raised daughter Mia, now 19, and son Flynn, 15. Mia was a keen netball player but is now concentrating on her studies at Edinburgh University, while Flynn is a talented cricketer.

Southgate enjoys his semi-rural surroundings, where he is usually out in the fresh air, walking the family's dogs as well as heading off on lengthy runs. His father Clive was a coach at Crawley Athletic Club, for whom the young Gareth competed, chiefly as a middle-distance runner, before concentrating full-time on football. And if coaching was in the family genes, then so was Southgate's second-most noticeable trait – an

appreciation of fine tailoring. The England manager's famous waistcoat is a nod to his maternal grandfather, Arthur Toll, a former Marine who was well known for his immaculate dress sense.

That formal attire is typical of Southgate's personality. He is, at heart, an old-school English gent. This Englishman's home is his castle, his manners are impeccable, and he is modest to such an extent that, during the World Cup, he genuinely hated the personal – rather than professional – adulation that was being heaped upon him. He loves drinking pints of Young's bitter and watching cricket, and is fired by a quiet determination to transform the battered image of English footballers and coaches.

Since its previous golden summer of Euro 96 – when Baddiel and Skinner's 'Three Lions' anthem insisted that 'Football's Coming Home', and Southgate played a starring role before missing the crucial penalty against Germany – Englishmen in professional football had fallen seriously out of fashion. The Premier League is packed with foreign managers and players, while the national team staggered from one embarrassment to the next. Since Terry Venables' success in reaching the semi-finals of the European Championships in 1996, England's native managers have proven particularly disastrous. We've had Kevin Keegan resigning in the Wembley toilets, Steve McClaren's 'wally with the brolly' routine, Roy Hodgson's humiliation by Iceland and Sam Allardyce being forced out for mouthing off to undercover reporters while drinking wine from a pint glass.

When England managers have quit in recent years, their decisions have usually impacted on Southgate. In 2006, when Sven-Göran Eriksson was replaced by McClaren, Southgate was the Middlesbrough captain who stepped up and accepted his first managerial job at the age of 35 – and without the coaching badges he needed. When Fabio Capello jumped ship in 2012, the FA asked Southgate – then their 'head of elite development' – to act as caretaker for an upcoming friendly against Holland. Southgate refused, and Stuart Pearce accepted the caretaker's job on a one-off basis. Then when Hodgson quit after the debacle of Euro 2016, the FA asked Southgate about taking over as a caretaker manager, but he was not interested in clearing up the mess in what he considered a 'no-win' situation.

He had previously turned down the post of FA technical director in 2012, instead leaving the governing body for a year and acting as good cop to Roy Keane's bad cop on ITV's football punditry team. When Southgate headed back to the FA as Under-21 boss in 2013, he was determined to improve relationships with the major clubs and to

THE ENGLAND MANAGER'S FAMOUS WAISTCOAT IS A NOD TO HIS MATERNAL GRANDFATHER, ARTHUR TOLL, A FORMER MARINE WHO WAS WELL KNOWN FOR HIS IMMACULATE DRESS SENSE.

achieve a joined-up approach with all of England's age-group teams. He was instrumental in setting up the system that brought World Cup glory to England's Under-17 and Under-20 teams in 2017. These successes were a clear indication that the FA was beginning to get things right in the way it prepared for and tackled tournaments. Southgate's own godson, Freddie Woodman – son and fellow goalkeeper to his friend Andy – helped the Under-20s triumph.

Yet despite all Southgate's influential work behind the scenes, his appointment in place of Allardyce was greeted with a mixture of yawns and jeers. The English public was disconnected from its national team and few believed that this so-called 'Yes man', 'stuffed blazer' and 'safe pair of hands' was the person to get things rolling again.

How wrong they turned out to be. Even while England were qualifying for the World Cup with relative comfort but little excitement, Southgate's revolution was under way. Wayne Rooney, the nation's captain and record goalscorer, was frozen out after a wedding-crashing drinking session at the team hotel. While Rooney's official international retirement did not arrive until August 2017, Southgate had effectively made the decision for him nine months earlier. Fellow 'big beasts' such as Jack Wilshere and Joe Hart were also jettisoned.

Then came the key decision to rip up England's formation and employ a ball-playing back three, wing-backs, one midfield 'pivot', two 'No. 8s' and Raheem Sterling behind Harry Kane. This tactical switch worked a treat in six unbeaten warm-up friendlies and was the template for a glorious run in Russia. A kind draw that pitted England against Tunisia and Panama – as well as the much-fancied Belgians – certainly helped. But England's manager travelled to Russia with a quiet confidence that this team was ready to end a cycle of failure. Few believed England were capable of going all the way (to the final week), when a succession of players claimed they were heading to Russia aiming to win the thing. Yet Southgate was always positive, and he sent a grateful nation into ecstasy.

The 'Yes man' had become a 'Yes! Yes! Oh God, Yes!' man.

ENGLAND'S WORLD CUP ADVENTURES

Brazil 1950

The World Cup had been going for 20 years before England even kicked a ball in the tournament. The Football Association thought entering tournaments against lesser nations was unworthy of the founder of modern football. We finally played in our first FIFA World Cup finals in 1950 in Brazil, where we were favourites to win Group 2.

After easily beating Chile 2–0, with a goal from Stan Mortensen in the first half and Wilf Mannion's header from a cross by Tom Finney in the second, over-confident England lost 1–0 to the USA's part-timers thanks to a freak deflected goal by Haitian-born Joe Gaetjens. England – with future manager Alf Ramsey at full-back – hit the woodwork 11 times. Mannion recalled: 'Our lads were dejected and humiliated. They just couldn't believe it. The shock of it.'

To go through, England needed to beat Spain and for Chile to beat the USA. Chile won, but Spain beat us 1–0, with a goal by Telmo Zarra. FA selection committee chairman Arthur Drewry said: 'I am speechless. We have learned a valuable lesson – the need for coaching in English football.'

Switzerland 1954

England's oldest-surviving player, Ivor Broadis – now aged 95 – lined up in the team that travelled to Switzerland for only our second World Cup finals. Broadis and Nat Lofthouse scored two goals each in the opening match – a 4–4 draw against Belgium. After beating hosts Switzerland 2–0 in searing heat three days later, they topped their group to reach the quarter-finals. But they had not been impressive. *The Times* reported: 'England, in a world sense, represent a Third Division side that has found its way into the last eight of the FA Cup. They must start thinking intelligently.' Sure enough, defending champions Uruguay beat us 4–2, helped by two terrible errors by goalkeeper Gil Merrick, who would never play for his country again.

West Germany beat hot favourites Hungary 3–2 in the final, and FA secretary Sir Stanley Rous announced a four-year coaching plan after England's exit, promising: 'We will introduce pinpoint passing, close marking and sharp shooting. The aim now is to win the 1958 World Cup.'

Sweden 1958

Just months before the World Cup finals, four England players – Manchester United's Roger Byrne, Duncan Edwards, David Pegg and Tommy Taylor – were killed in the Munich air disaster.

Another rising star from Old Trafford, Bobby Charlton, cheated death in the disaster and he was included in the England squad. However, despite calls from the media to play him, he wasn't given a single minute's action in Sweden. At the end of the group stage, the Soviet Union and England were tied. England lost 1–0 in the play-off to decide the second-placed team in the group and went out. At least England were the only team not to lose to the eventual winners Brazil, after a 0–0 draw. England coach Walter Winterbottom said: 'We had extraordinary bad luck and our finishing was poor.'

Chile 1962

In Chile, England came second in their group, and in the quarter-finals lost 3–1 to defending champions Brazil, including two goals from inspirational winger Garrincha. The defeat signalled the end for coach Walter Winterbottom, who retired after leading England to four World Cup finals. He said: 'We would have had to have lifted our game to the highest state of our potential to have beaten Brazil.'

Later that year Alf Ramsey became England manager. Crucially, he insisted that he, rather than a committee of selectors, would choose the team.

England 1966

World Cup fever gripped the country, with matches at top First Division grounds, but England made the most of playing all their games in the national stadium. Crowds at Wembley saw England draw 0–0 in the opening game against Uruguay, before beating both Mexico and France 2–0 to reach the quarter-finals, where we overcame Argentina 1–0 before knocking out Portugal 2–1 in the semis.

On that unbelievable day, Saturday 30 July 1966, mighty West Germany stood between captain Bobby Moore's heroic team and the World Cup. After a late German equaliser in normal time, England took a 3–2 lead in extra-time with Geoff Hurst's controversial second goal, which was judged to have crossed the line. In the final moments of the match Hurst powered home his third, for England to win 4–2. 'They think it's all over . . . it is now!' Hurst became the only player to score a hat-trick in a World Cup Final. The Queen presented the Jules Rimet Trophy to Moore, who held football's greatest prize aloft.

England manager Alf Ramsey – who had predicted victory – said: 'I was a little worried that our football was still behind other international teams. From the fact we have won the World Cup, I think it can be taken that we have caught up.'

Mexico 1970

As champions, England automatically qualified and, after a narrow 1–0 group stage defeat to Brazil – which saw Gordon Banks's Save of the Century from Pelé – they again met West Germany, this time in the quarter-final. First-choice goalkeeper Banks had food poisoning, so a nervous Peter Bonetti played instead. Goals by Alan Mullery and Martin Peters put England in a commanding position. But Franz Beckenbauer led a comeback and, with the inspirational Bobby Charlton substituted, Gerd Müller's extra-time goal gave Germany a 3–2 win.

Hero of 1966, midfielder Alan Ball said: 'It wouldn't be so bad if we had lost to a great team today, but the Germans were nothing.' Brazil went on to win the cup for the third time, and to keep the trophy.

West Germany 1974

England did not get to the World Cup finals after failing to beat Poland in the last qualifier at Wembley in October 1973. An inspired performance by Polish goalkeeper Jan Tomaszewski – dubbed 'The Clown' by Brian Clough – earned a 1–1 draw, despite 35 England attempts on goal and 26 corners.

Manager Sir Alf Ramsey said: 'You have seen a great team performance by England. I do not think we could have played better. In life, one has many disappointments. The players played so well and have nothing to show for it.' Ramsey was sacked months later.

Franz Beckenbauer lifted the glittering new World Cup trophy for West Germany on home soil, beating Johan Cruyff's brilliant Holland 2–1 in the Final. England had fallen behind the rest of the world by the end of Ramsey's 12-year reign and the FA turned to Don Revie, the successful Leeds boss, to revive the team's fortunes. But his reign soon ran into problems as the Three Lions failed to make it to the final stages of the 1976 European Championships. As it turned out, he wouldn't even see out the 1978 World Cup qualifying campaign.

Argentina 1978

Italy stopped us reaching the finals in Argentina under new manager Ron Greenwood, who took over when Don Revie sensationally quit. Goals from Antognoni and Bettega saw Italy beat us in Rome in 1976. Despite a Kevin Keegan-inspired 2–0 revenge at Wembley a year later, the Italians scored more against minnows Luxembourg and Finland to qualify ahead of us.

Greenwood pointed a finger at the culture of too many club matches and putting results above quality. He said: 'This has been the ruination of English football, and the public have been largely to blame for demanding it.' England fans had to watch Scotland instead – but despite boss Ally MacLeod's prophecy of victory, the Scots lost to Peru, drew with Iran and went home, even though they famously beat Holland 3–2.

Spain 1982

Inspired by midfield powerhouse Bryan Robson's 27th-second opening goal in a 3–1 win against France, England next beat Czechoslovakia 2–0 and Kuwait 1–0. In the second group stage, England drew 0–0 with West Germany, so they needed to beat Spain by two goals. With minutes to go, England sent on unfit Kevin Keegan and Trevor Brooking for their World Cup finals debuts. Keegan's header went agonisingly close. But the match ended goalless, and we were out. Bobby Robson was named as the retiring Greenwood's successor.

Greenwood said: 'The only thing we didn't do was score goals at the right time. Our main failing was a lack of inventiveness.'

FA chairman Sir Bert Millichip said: 'I would hope that eventually we can introduce greater skills into the England team. This can only happen if we get it right at school and youth level and it is about this that we will have detailed discussions with Bobby Robson. We would be foolish if we did not sit down and look at the whole England situation.'

Mexico 1986

England started badly, losing 1–0 to Portugal and drawing 0–0 with Morocco. It was win or bust against Poland, but Gary Lineker's hat-trick took us to a last-16 tie with Paraguay. A 3–0 win meant a quarter-final against Argentina – bitter rivals after the 1982 Falklands War.

Diego Maradona scored his first goal thanks to the infamous 'Hand of God' – a handball the ref failed to spot. His second was genius – dribbling past five England players and keeper Peter Shilton. Gary Lineker pulled one back before time was up. Manager Bobby Robson said: 'I won't be resigning. We have gone out to a dubious goal and to one of the best teams in the tournament.'

Robson survived calls for his head after losing all three group games at Euro 88, guiding England to qualification for Italia 90. This would be his swansong before joining PSV Eindhoven. Few predicted how successful it would be.

Italy 1990

England's finest hour since 1966. After beating Belgium 1–0 (thanks to David Platt's injury-time volley) and Cameroon 3–2 in the knockout stages, we reached the semi-finals – and faced West Germany again. Level after extra time, it came down to penalties. Although Peter Shilton dived the right way for every penalty, he was unable to save any. German goalkeeper Bodo Illgner managed to save England's fourth penalty, taken by Stuart Pearce. Olaf Thon then scored for Germany. Chris Waddle would have to score and hope that Shilton saved Germany's fifth penalty. But Waddle missed completely, sending England out, accompanied by our new hero Paul 'Gazza' Gascoigne in tears.

Manager Bobby Robson said: 'We get told we play old-fashioned, medieval football but we have shown everyone that our game isn't like that at all.'

USA 1994

Did we not like that. Under former Watford boss Graham Taylor, England had their worst campaign yet and failed to reach the finals. A disappointing 1–1 draw with Norway at Wembley and a 2–0 collapse in Oslo was followed by double Dutch disaster. At Wembley a 2–0 lead was squandered and in Rotterdam Ronald Koeman scored the first in a 2–0 win – four minutes after he should have been sent off for fouling David Platt as he went through on goal. Even San Marino went ahead nine seconds into our final qualifier before we finally won 7–1. It was irrelevant. That night, Holland beat Poland to qualify along with Norway.

Taylor quit, saying: 'No one can grasp the depths of my personal disappointment.' Hotshots Bebeto and Romario led Brazil to their country's fourth win.

France 1998

With Glenn Hoddle in charge, England beat Tunisia 2–0, lost 2–1 to Romania and beat Colombia 2–0 to meet former winners Argentina in the last 16. A fiery game began with two penalties – converted by Batistuta and Shearer. Then 18-year-old Michael Owen's brilliant strike was cancelled out by Zanetti. But David Beckham was controversially red-carded in the 47th minute for a petulant kick on Diego Simeone, who had fouled him then ruffled his hair. Brave England finally lost on penalties after a 2–2 draw. Beckham received death threats.

Hoddle said: 'It's a bitter pill to take. We're distraught. The sending-off cost us the game. But even with ten men we defended like lions.'

Argentina coach Daniel Passarella gloated: 'It's very sweet to send the English back home, very sweet.'

South Korea/Japan 2002

A 1–1 draw with Sweden, a sweet 1–0 victory over Argentina – thanks to a David Beckham penalty – and a 0–0 draw with Nigeria took Sven-Göran Eriksson's England out of their group. A solid 3–0 defeat of Denmark meant a quarter-final against favourites Brazil in Shizuoka, Japan. Despite falling behind to a Michael Owen goal, Ronaldinho inspired Brazil, setting up Rivaldo's equaliser, then bamboozled keeper David Seaman with a free-kick that sailed 42 yards, going in over his head. Brazil went on to win the World Cup.

England captain Beckham – who had broken his foot before the tournament – said: 'I honestly felt we would have won the World Cup if we'd got past Brazil. Now the 2006 World Cup is a genuine target for us.'

Germany 2006

With their party-loving WAGS in a hotel nearby, England's players had a jittery start to Eriksson's second World Cup finals, beating Paraguay 1–0, Trinidad and Tobago 2–0, and drawing 2–2 with Sweden to top Group C. A narrow 1–0 win over Ecuador set up a quarter-final against Portugal. After 67 minutes Wayne Rooney was sent off for stamping on Ricardo Carvalho, then argued with his Manchester United team-mate Cristiano Ronaldo – who winked at the Portugal bench as Rooney walked. Ten-man England hung on for penalties but were gutted as Ricardo saved shots from Frank Lampard, Steven Gerrard and Jamie Carragher to put us out.

It was Eriksson's final match. He said: 'We can't blame the referee or somebody else. These players should have at least been in the final.'

The FA turned to Eriksson's assistant Steve McClaren, who left his job with Middlesbrough for a shot at the ultimate challenge. It soon went wrong for McClaren, though, as the Three Lions failed to make it to Euro 2008. With morale at rock bottom, FA chiefs decided to put England's fate in the hands of another foreign boss.

South Africa 2010

England's Italian manager Fabio Capello led the Golden Generation's final tilt at the World Cup – and saw the dream slip away horribly. Goalkeeper Robert Green's opening-match howler handed the USA a 1–1 draw, we drew 0–0 with Algeria, then edged into the knockout stage by beating Slovenia 1–0. Germany gave us our worst World Cup hammering in Bloemfontein. But goal-line technology might have changed everything. With Germany 2–1 up, Frank Lampard's dipping volley hit the bar and bounced a yard over the line. Keeper Manuel Neuer grabbed the ball, played on and the goal was not given. England collapsed to a 4–1 defeat.

Like Ron Greenwood years earlier, Capello blamed the long English season, saying: 'All the players were tired. They didn't play like the players we know.'

Brazil 2014

Roy Hodgson's England gave their worst performance in a World Cup finals, losing 2–1 to Italy – inspired by Andrea Pirlo's passing – and Uruguay, led by their brilliant bad-boy striker Luis Suárez. We were out after just two group games. Could it get worse? Oh, yes. The third game, against group winners Costa Rica, ended goalless, leaving England bottom with their lowest points total ever in a group.

Hodgson said: 'I am numb with sadness. So many hopes and dreams and so much work has been blown away. I don't have any intention to resign. I've been really happy with the way the players have responded to the work we've done. I'm bitterly disappointed but I don't feel I need to resign. If the FA think I'm not the right man to do the job, that will be their decision, not mine.' Roy stayed on . . . to oversee our European Championships defeat by Iceland two years later. Only one team had a more painful World Cup – hosts and favourites Brazil, humiliated 7–1 in the semi-final by eventual champions Germany.

QUALIFIERS: THE ROAD TO RUSSIA

To appreciate the transformation of this England team and to remind ourselves of the previous disconnect between fans and players, we have to rewind to the opening games of the qualifying campaign.

First, 4 September 2016. It is the 94th minute of the first Group F match in the Slovakian city of Trnava, and England are delivering a pedestrian, colourless and underwhelming performance against 10 men in the first game of World Cup qualifying. The opening game of the Sam Allardyce era is not going to plan. The 1,800 supporters who made the trip are wondering why they bothered. Harry Kane's hangover from Euro 2016 has continued and he has been replaced by Daniel Sturridge. Wayne Rooney has now become England's most-capped outfield player but has been playing in the controversial deeper midfield role that he occupied in France.

Yet in the fifth minute of injury time, Adam Lallana chooses an absolutely vital moment to force the ball into the net for his first ever goal and we have lift-off. Sort of. Because by the time Lallana finally scored a goal for his country, groaning England fans in pubs had turned their backs on the TV and those at home had switched channels. It appeared nothing had really changed from the Iceland game, other than a new bloke in charge of the team. No journalist who was covering the game could have imagined at this point that Allardyce would never manage his country again. And not even the most optimistic of England supporters – and they have become almost an extinct breed – would have predicted the air miles some Three Lions fans would clock up on a fantasy ride to the last week of a major tournament.

But by the time Malta arrived at Wembley on 8 October, Allardyce had been sent packing from his 'dream job' and Gareth Southgate installed as caretaker. A staggering 81,000 fans flocked to Wembley to watch a team ranked 176th in the world get defeated 2–0 by England. The scorers were Daniel Sturridge and Dele Alli, who played well as a No. 10. Jesse Lingard was a starter for his first England cap and the team wasted loads of chances.

The next game, a trip to Slovenia on 11 October, was significant for a terrific performance by a player who did not even make the final 23 – Joe Hart. He twice denied Josip Iličić after poor back passes from Eric Dier and Jordan Henderson, and delivered a brilliant, acrobatic save when turning Jasmin Kurti's header onto the crossbar. Despite drawing away from home, England were poor, with Rooney having been relegated to the subs' bench. His time as an international was coming to an end.

The most eagerly anticipated group game was Scotland at home on 11 November. Man-of-the-match Sturridge, Lallana and Gary Cahill scored a trio of headers in a 3–0 win, which would prove to be Rooney's last game. In Southgate's fourth and final match as interim manager, Spain arrived for a friendly on 16 November. It was a decent audition for the job as manager, with England playing well. Lallana and Jamie Vardy scored, while the Spanish grabbed two goals at the end for a 2–2 draw. Aaron Cresswell landed his first cap, with Nathaniel Clyne, Theo Walcott, Phil Jagielka and Andros Townsend playing their final games, for the time being at least.

Southgate was appointed permanent manager a couple of weeks later, and in his first game afterwards England faced Germany in another friendly on 22 March 2017 in Dortmund. Crucially, Southgate

NOT EVEN THE MOST OPTIMISTIC OF ENGLAND SUPPORTERS WOULD HAVE PREDICTED THE AIR MILES SOME THREE LIONS FANS WOULD CLOCK UP ON THE FANTASY RIDE TO THE LAST WEEK OF A MAJOR TOURNAMENT.

experimented with a three-man defence, and England played well early on, although Lukas Podolski celebrated his last international appearance with a stunning winner. Michael Keane, James Ward-Prowse and Nathan Redmond won their first caps, and some of the England fans let themselves and their country down with vile anti-German chanting.

Four days later, it was back to qualifying and a 2–0 win over Lithuania at Wembley. Jermain Defoe and Vardy scored in a dull contest that will be remembered for a perfectly observed minute's silence for the Westminster terror attack, and terminally ill Sunderland fan Bradley Lowery, 5, leading England out with his friend Defoe.

Unsurprisingly, the national anthems were not respectfully observed when England headed north of the border to face Scotland in Glasgow on 10 June. The game had a frantic finish and unimpressive England's blushes were spared by a late equaliser. A 70th-minute goal from Alex Oxlade-Chamberlain nudged Southgate's side towards victory but Leigh Griffiths scored two free-kicks in the 87th and 90th minutes – with Hart at fault – to send Hampden Park bonkers. Kane bailed out England, not for the last time, with a difficult finish to level three minutes into injury time.

The team travelled to Paris three days later for a friendly with France and lost 3–2 against 10 men, with Kane scoring twice. Southgate claimed we saw the good and bad of England; at times his side were completely outplayed and it felt as though the Three Lions were going backwards. Kieran Trippier earned his first cap and subsequently played a big part in taking the team forward.

But these were still unsettling times. England beat Malta 4–0 on 1 September but only after a flurry of late goals from Ryan Bertrand, Danny Welbeck and a second for Kane. When Bertrand made it 2–0 in the 86th minute, some of the travelling fans had left for the island's bars, and as Southgate revealed before the World Cup, his players received verbal abuse from fans on the team bus.

Three days later, England moved within two points of qualifying, courtesy of a 2–1 win over Slovakia. Eric Dier and the impressive Marcus Rashford scored after the team had been given a scare when the Slovaks took a third-minute lead. Southgate's side were poor in the first half, but they showed character and dug themselves out of a hole.

And so, on 5 October, England qualified with a game to spare, but it was not impressive. In fact, it was pretty boring. So dull, indeed, that on the night England booked their place on the plane to Russia, the fans at Wembley threw paper aeroplanes onto the pitch to relieve the tedium. Kane sealed top spot in Group F with a 94th-minute strike after a cracking cross from Kyle Walker.

The final game against Lithuania in Vilnius on 8 October was always going to be an anti-climax. It was another dismal performance and Kane settled this game on an artificial pitch from the penalty spot. Had Lithuania taken their chances they would have won, but plus points were international debuts for Harry Maguire and Harry Winks

After 10 games, England finished top with 26 points, eight points clear of Slovakia in second place. The campaign ended in victory through mediocrity, and it was at this moment Southgate decided to change his tactics, bring in a permanent three-man defence and virtually start again. The December draw in Moscow seemed kind but no one, not even Southgate himself, could ever have expected the tournament to unfold like it did.

POSITION	TEAM	PLAYED	WON	DRAWN	LOST	FOR	AGAINST	GD	POINTS
1	ENGLAND	10	8	2	0	18	3	15	26
2	SLOVAKIA	10	6	0	4	17	7	10	18
3	SCOTLAND	10	5	3	2	17	12	5	18
4	SLOVENIA	10	4	3	3	12	7	5	15
5	LITHUANIA	10	1	3	6	7	20	-13	6
6	MALTA	10	0	1	9	3	25	-22	1

A SQUAD OF YOUNG LIONS

Gareth Southgate put the dreams of the nation in the hands of his young lions. When he named his 23-man World Cup squad on 16 May, it was the third-youngest in history – behind 1958 and 2006 – with an average age of 26 years and 18 days. Seventeen of them were not even born the last time England won a World Cup quarter-final, against Cameroon in 1990. It was also the second-least-experienced England squad, with an average of just 20 caps each. Only the 1962 squad in Chile had fewer.

Southgate's trust in these rookies, many of whom he'd mentored through England's junior set-up, was a bold and brave call. He defended his picks, saying: 'I believe this is a squad we can be excited about. It is a young group but with some really important senior players, so I feel the balance is good, in terms of experience, character and also positional balance. We have a lot of energy and athleticism but also players that are equally comfortable in possession of the ball. I think people can see the style of play we've been looking to develop.'

Uncapped Liverpool defender Trent Alexander-Arnold, 19, was a surprise choice as he was handed his first call-up. The young right-back played in the Champions League Final against Real Madrid in Kiev before joining up with England, making it a remarkable end to the season for the talented teenager. There was also a place for Chelsea midfielder Ruben Loftus-Cheek, 22, who spent the season on loan at Crystal Palace and impressed Southgate with his powerful performances. Leicester City defender Harry Maguire, 25, was at the Euro 2016 tournament – but as a fan, not a player. And then Manchester United's converted left-back Ashley Young, 32 at the time of his call-up, brought some crucial experience along with Chelsea's solid, dependable centre-back Gary Cahill, also 32.

Southgate needed these reliable characters, as the squad's inexperience, especially behind that defence, was an obvious concern. Keepers Jordan Pickford, Jack Butland and Nick Pope had just nine caps between them.

The England players could not hide their excitement after being told they had been picked. Young posted a picture of himself as a child

> **'WE HAVE A LOT OF ENERGY AND ATHLETICISM BUT ALSO PLAYERS THAT ARE EQUALLY COMFORTABLE IN POSSESSION OF THE BALL.'**
> GARETH SOUTHGATE

wearing an England shirt, with the comment: 'Maybe this picture said I was gonna live my dream and go to a World Cup – dreams do come true.' Alexander-Arnold said: 'Dreamt of going to a World Cup since I was a kid. Today that dream came true, an honour to represent the Three Lions!' United's Marcus Rashford wrote an emotional message to his mum, saying: 'After years of you standing on the touchline in the cold and rain, Mum we're off to the World Cup!' Defender Kyle Walker posted a screenshot of a missed call from Southgate, writing: 'One call you don't want to miss!'

A World Cup quarter-final, where England were expected to meet Germany or Brazil, was the FA's unofficial target for the tournament. FA President Prince William wished them luck when he visited the squad at their St George's Park training camp in Staffordshire, where he chatted to Southgate and captain Harry Kane, and presented Alexander-Arnold with his No. 22 shirt.

Nobody, at Wembley at least, was making demands of Southgate's team to win the trophy this time. Their achievement in Russia surpassed all expectations – and the squad returned as heroes. Like Sir Alf Ramsey's legendary England side of 1966, their names will be remembered for decades to come.

'I BELIEVE THIS IS A SQUAD WE CAN BE EXCITED ABOUT.'
GARETH SOUTHGATE

JORDAN PICKFORD

GOALKEEPER

Age: 24

England caps: 10

England goals: 0

Club: Everton

Jordan Pickford's first World Cup memory is of going to school and talking about Ronaldinho's freak long-range free-kick winner. That was back in 2002 when England were dumped out by Brazil at the quarter-final stage with an iconic goal that left David Seaman in floods of tears. So from the age of eight, well before he became a star in Russia, Pickford knew all about the spotlight that comes with being No. 1 for the Three Lions.

Back in those days Pickford was also useful in a different kind of gloves. He trained at Washington Boxing Club in his home town and impressed with his work in the ring. But it was his goalkeeping that caught the eye of Sunderland, and he joined them as a schoolboy. Then, years later, Gareth Southgate turned to Pickford to succeed Joe Hart because his excellent distribution meant he could play an important part in England's new passing style, as well as keeping the ball out of the net with his shot-stopping ability.

And being good on the deck started in those early days at the Academy of Light when Pickford would sometimes play outfield. 'Back in the day I held my own when I played outfield for my school,' he said. 'I played a couple of games out when I was younger for Sunderland. The dreaded left-back role! Kevin Ball would put us up at centre-back to get a picture of how it was in front of me, so I thought that worked well. I think he said I was the best centre-half at the time. He's a Sunderland ledge, so I'll take that.'

Pickford was seen as a keeper with huge potential at Sunderland, but he did his growing up during a period of loans. The road to Russia started with a loan spell at Darlington. He was then sent to Alfreton Town, where his first away game was against a Wrexham team of seasoned campaigners like Brett Ormerod, Glen Little and Dele Adebola trying to show him up. At the time, his team-mates were stunned that this teenager was yelling at them like his hero Peter Schmeichel did at Manchester United. 'I remember at Wrexham they put seven players on top of me at corners,' he said. 'The first one I could have come and got it, the second

1

'YOU CAN'T BE FRIGHTENED AS YOU ONLY GET ONE CHANCE. I'VE ALWAYS TAKEN THAT CHANCE WELL.'

one I came and took it. And they ran away. You can't be frightened as you only get one chance. I've always taken that chance and taken it well. At Darlington I was just coming for crosses. Being confident but not arrogant is the key. I was confident in my ability and in my bravery.'

When Pickford talks, his confidence shines through. Nothing seems to faze him despite being a youngster in goalkeeping terms. By 22 he was a Premier League regular after earning his stripes away from the top flight, with loans down as far as non-league. His rise since breaking through to the first team at the Stadium of Light has been meteoric, with Everton willing to pay £30 million to take him to Goodison Park.

Pickford was pulling into his mother's driveway back in 2016 when he received the news of a first England call-up. His mum Sue did not believe it at the time, but her lad just begun the journey that would lead to Russia. Tom Heaton had picked up a minor injury ahead of a qualifier in Slovenia, and Southgate called up a keeper he knew so well from the Under-21s. His first start came just eight months before England's amazing experience in the World Cup, when he became a hero of the knockout stages. Speaking about his debut, he admitted: 'You can't let it faze you too much because that is when you put pressure on yourself – I've never put pressure on myself before. Even making my debut at Wembley against Germany – and it was sold out, 90,000 – that was new to me, but I embraced it and used that atmosphere to make me better.'

At the World Cup, Pickford looked nailed on for a starting place when Southgate handed him the No. 1 jersey as he dished out the squad numbers. His family travelled over to watch him in Russia, along with his fiancée, childhood sweetheart Megan Davison. The pair have been together since they were teenagers and her father's reaction to Pickford's heroics went viral on social media.

England's backroom staff had him studying opponents – right down to the history of their penalty takers – and making sure preparations were spot-on for the tournament. But against Tunisia in England's opener, Wahbi Khazri did not take his side's spot-kick as he was Pickford's team-mate at Sunderland and had had a few penalties saved in training. Ashley Young ran over to the bench to get information on Ferjani Sassi, but Sassi had never taken a penalty before. Pickford dived the right way and got his fingertips to the ball, but it was the first goal he conceded at the finals.

In the first defeat to Belgium, he came so close to calamity when the ball squirmed through his hands and looked like trickling in. It needed Gary Cahill to clear off the line to spare his blushes. Adnan Januzaj scored the winner in that game and it led to comments from Thibaut Courtois, who suggested that Pickford would have saved it if he had been taller.

But the England keeper got the last laugh with his penalty heroics against Colombia in the last 16. England had practised everything, right down to the walk from the centre circle and the way Pickford rattled the bar with his gloves every time a Colombian steadied himself in the run-up. The result was a stunning save from Carlos Bacca and a memorable first World Cup shoot-out victory for England.

Then came his three saves against Sweden, with one from Marcus Berg getting scooped away from the bottom corner and earning comparisons with Gordon Banks's heroics against Brazil in 1970. Pickford said: 'It's all about the crucial timing of a save but it's also being in the right position at the right time. And that's what we focus on in training. We do about 600 saves a week just to make one save on a Saturday, and that's what it's all about.'

Pickford picked up a bizarre thumb injury punching himself in that game, but there was no lasting damage. And no danger of him losing his status as a World Cup hero.

KYLE WALKER

Born to an English mother and Jamaican father in Sheffield, Walker grew up on a council estate in the city and started playing football aged seven. He nearly quit at 15 but stuck with it thanks to advice from his mum, Tracey. She doesn't usually watch him play as she gets too nervous, but she would help out by staying at home and giving directions over the phone when dad Michael got lost on the way back from matches.

Kyle himself is now a dad of three – Roman, 6, Riaan, 2, and Reign, 9 months – with his girlfriend of nine years, Annie Kilner.

If there is one player who was the key to England's success in the 2018 World Cup, it may well have been Walker. Not so much for what he did on the pitch – although his tireless work was pretty impressive, given he was playing out of position as a third centre-half – but because Walker was the one who linked together the two biggest club representations in the squad: Spurs and Manchester City. Ex-Spurs team-mates, especially Eric Dier and Dele Alli, shared banter with him on social media and in the England hotel. He was able to tell his Etihad colleagues just what decent blokes he had left behind at Tottenham, giving Kane, Dier and other Spurs players the same message about his new team-mates.

Normally a full-back for club and country, in Russia he looked, perhaps for the first time, genuinely at home in an England shirt. He is one of the shorter men in the side, at 5ft 10, and time and again he used his renowned speed and agility to get himself and the team out of trouble. Although his delivery may not match Trippier's, Walker is arguably England's best right-back.

CENTRE-BACK / RIGHT-BACK

Age: 28

England caps: 40

England goals: 0

Club: Manchester City

2

DANNY ROSE

LEFT-BACK

Age: 28

England caps: 22

England goals: 0

Club: Tottenham Hotspur

3

Left-back Danny comes from a family immersed in football. Born in Doncaster to Jamaican parents, his younger brother Mitch plays for Grimsby and he is the cousin of York City striker Michael Rankine. Michael's uncle Mark played for Sheffield United and Tranmere Rovers.

Having suffered racist abuse during a game six years ago, Rose made the decision to tell his parents not to attend the World Cup in case they too were on the receiving end. 'I don't want them coming out to Russia because I'm worried about their safety,' he said. But he changed his mind during the tournament after the reception for England's players and fans proved so positive.

The 5ft 8in star recently revealed he's been battling depression and that football has been his salvation. Rose's bravery in speaking out summed up the feel of Southgate's England. The Spurs star felt sufficiently secure within the squad to open up about the condition that has followed him for more than a year as he has battled injury.

Rose's strength of character was clear last summer when he spoke about his anger at Spurs and the club's transfer policies. The former Leeds kid – whom Chelsea tried and failed to snare as a 17-year-old – paid his dues in loan spells at Watford, Peterborough, Bristol City and Sunderland.

But despite having been at Spurs for 11 years – and announcing himself with a stunning volley against Arsenal in 2010 – he has made just 118 Premier League appearances for the club. This season he was sidelined in favour of Ben Davies, although Spurs insiders are adamant that Mauricio Pochettino likes the fact that Rose shakes things up as a matter of course.

ERIC DIER

MIDFIELDER/DEFENDER

Age: 24

England caps: 31

England goals: 3

Club: Tottenham Hotspur

4

No matter what happens in the future, Eric Dier will always be remembered as the first England player to score the winning goal in a World Cup penalty shoot-out. Born in Cheltenham, and the grandson of former FA secretary Ted Croker, he grew up in Portugal from the age of seven with his parents, former tennis pro Jeremy and Louise, who works in hospitality.

The family had moved there for a better life and job opportunities. In 2010, his mum and dad returned to England but Eric remained in Portugal, living at the academy of Sporting Lisbon, one of the nation's highest-profile football teams. He made his name as a player of great potential while in the city, and met his girlfriend Maria Hansen there just before signing for Spurs.

Bookworm Eric loves art galleries and political debate. And his football development has been equally impressive. While on the books of Sporting Lisbon he was appearing regularly in England age-group sides, despite a difficult 18-month loan spell at Everton.

A £4-million move to Spurs in 2014 saw him score the winning goal on his debut, in virtually the final touch of the game from a pass by substitute Harry Kane at West Ham. Dier began at Spurs as a right-back but was switched to a central role by Mauricio Pochettino, and it was the move into midfield as Tottenham made an unexpected title challenge in the 2015–16 season that saw him promoted into the England reckoning.

Dier's late header completed a stunning comeback win in Berlin against Germany ahead of Euro 2016, and his superb free-kick should have brought victory over Russia in the tournament opener. But the Spurs man suffered like the rest of Roy Hodgson's side in France, and was forced off ill at half-time in the Iceland debacle.

JOHN STONES

Unlikely goal hero John was dubbed the 'quietest and most sporty' kid at Penistone Grammar School in South Yorkshire, where the motto is 'Never Stop Flying'. But his initial love was golf, not football, and he was a gifted player as a junior. John says parents Janet and Peter kept him grounded when he left school at 16. He signed for Barnsley and was paid £500 a week, and according to Stones his parents 'came to every game, home and away'.

Stones did not always have it easy at Manchester City last season, as he struggled with injury, and question marks were raised about his form. Club boss Pep Guardiola wanted to get him ready for the World Cup and Stones was fit in time to feature for City in May, confident in the knowledge that if he remained injury-free he would be a vital figure in Southgate's plan to play three centre-backs. Stones was a starter in both England friendlies leading up to the finals and was nailed on to be in the first team alongside his brothers-in-arms, Kyle Walker and Harry Maguire. The boy from Barnsley epitomised a team that came from humble roots.

In Russia, England proved particularly adept at set-pieces and Stones was crucial to that, although he even surprised himself by scoring two in the 6–1 demolition of Panama. And when it came to the rough-house encounter with Colombia he showed he could look after himself, although he did brand them 'the dirtiest team I've ever played against'. He added, 'It was a difficult situation to be in, but one that we overcame and can look back on and be very proud of.'

Stones lives with girlfriend Millie Savage in a six-bedroom home in Cheshire. They met at school when he was 12 and they have been together ever since. The 6ft 2in player has a tattoo of Millie on his arm.

CENTRE-BACK

Age: 24

England caps: 32

England goals: 2

Club: Manchester City

5

HARRY MAGUIRE

CENTRE-BACK

Age: 25

England caps: 11

England goals: 1

Club: Leicester City

6

He's the other Harry, but his heroics in Russia won the nation's heart after Kane had already sealed his place in history. Maguire, christened 'Slabhead' by his Leicester City team-mates, lived the dream in Russia, arguably more than any other member of Gareth Southgate's squad.

Two years earlier, he had gone out to France with his mates to cheer on Roy Hodgson's side as they flopped at Euro 2016. This summer, only nine months after making his debut in Lithuania, Maguire was one of the first names on the England team sheet.

Harry, who now makes £4 million a year playing for Leicester, shot to national fame after scoring with an electrifying header in the World Cup quarter-final victory over Sweden. But it has hardly been an instant success story for Sheffield-born Harry, another of the Yorkshire core in the Three Lions squad.

'When he first joined us, at 11, you could see he was one of our good players, but did I think he'd be playing in a World Cup quarter-final? Absolutely not,' says Martin McKee, head of PE at Harry's old school, St Mary's Catholic High School in Chesterfield. In fact, the Three Lions star was a straight-A student who his teachers believed was destined for a job far less glamorous.

'He was very capable academically. He got A* and A grades in his GCSEs,' said his old headteacher, Sue Cain. 'I think he would have gone on to study business or maths and probably have been an accountant.' As well as being gifted, Harry was as good as gold at school. 'He was never in any trouble and he had such a good attitude,' said Sue. 'He was a remarkable pupil who always came in and worked very hard.'

But his obsession with the Beautiful Game from a young age meant that Harry had other ideas for his future, and through sheer determination he made his boyhood dream a sparkling reality. He and his brothers, Joe, 27, and Laurence, 21, were encouraged to play by their father, Alan Maguire, 51, who is now a financial services director but used to play football semi-professionally, working his way up in the Co-operative Insurance Society. 'We were football-mad in the house,'

said Harry. He and his brothers would raucously play in the garden in precarious proximity to the house. 'I don't know how Mum coped at times,' he admitted. 'I'm sure there were plenty of broken windows.' Meanwhile his dad Alan bemoaned the churned-up lawn.

For Harry these were formative days. 'I was incredibly competitive, growing up with two brothers. We'd argue and play against each other in the garden continuously,' he said. 'We used to play hours of tennis and badminton. It was really competitive. Even when we do something in the garden now, we all want to win. We play head tennis over a net, and it's always ending up in arguments over whether the ball is in or out. If we have a competition, I want to beat them.'

The Maguires would all gather around the TV when England played at tournaments and Harry became a die-hard supporter of the national team. 'I can remember everyone having flags hanging out of their car windows during the World Cup,' he said. 'When I was growing up, I loved watching and learning from Rio Ferdinand and John Terry. Ferdinand had his pace, and used to step in and play a lot. Terry was brilliant and really good on the ball as well.'

There are pictures of Harry at Euro 2016, in Saint-Étienne, in with the fans. 'My mates were all out there, so I went and joined them for the game,' he said. 'Unfortunately it was the Slovakia one, the final group game. It ended up 0–0, but it was good to be over there, see all the fans, experience the atmosphere. The support was incredible. If I wasn't in the England squad I'd be watching it on TV, with all my mates, celebrating every goal. I'm definitely a supporter.'

Now, having played eleven games for England, Harry is the one being cheered on, and his brothers have also found football success. Joe Maguire plays part-time, Laurence plays for Chesterfield, who were relegated from the Football League last season, and Harry, of course, rose from Sheffield United to Hull City, Leicester City and England. Despite their varying levels of success in the sport and the friendly competition left over from their youth, there's no jealousy between the brothers. Joe and Laurence flew to Russia to support Harry as part of a huge contingent of family and friends.

Cool-headed Harry was as unshakeable before the tournament as he was during it. 'I don't think I'll stop taking risks,' he said. 'It's my way. I'm confident in my ability. Gareth Southgate is calm, his temperament is good, he rises above things. Tactically, he is really good. His philosophy is to be fearless. Gareth doesn't really fear anything. He's trying to put belief in the players that we can actually go there and cause a surprise.'

It seems not much has changed since Harry was a youngster. Travis Binnion, director of Sheffield's youth academy, said of Harry: 'As a kid, he was very confident on the pitch, but off it he was down-to-earth and quite reserved. He had the air that he knew best, but not in a big-headed way. He would listen, but he would back his ability to know the game, and he was very bright. You could see the cogs ticking in his head.'

His down-to-earth nature is encouraged by all of those around him. 'I still live a normal life,' he said. 'I make sacrifices in terms of alcohol and food, but I do jobs at home, stay as grounded as I can. That comes from my mum and dad, they expect it. They don't make any excuses for me. "You've got a game in a few days? No, go and do it [whatever job it may be]."'

There is one person, however, who is unapologetically his biggest fan. His long-term girlfriend, 25-year-old Fern Hawkins, posted gushing Instagram posts almost daily about her beau during the World Cup. 'I am so proud of you. You amaze me every single day,' wrote Fern, who's been with Harry for six years.

Maguire turned up for England duty carrying his kit in a bin bag. But although he's a grounded boy from Yorkshire, everyone agrees there is something special about Harry. Former youth coach John Pemberton perhaps sums it up best. 'He's a level-headed, ordinary Sheffield lad, from a really supportive background – but he's got an extraordinary presence.'

'IF I WASN'T IN THE ENGLAND SQUAD I'D BE WATCHING IT ON TV, WITH ALL MY MATES, CELEBRATING EVERY GOAL. I'M DEFINITELY A SUPPORTER.'

JESSE LINGARD

MIDFIELDER

Age: 25

England caps: 17

England goals: 2

Club: Manchester United

7

Before the World Cup, England's diminutive No. 7 tweeted the message, 'Just a little boy chasing a big dream' alongside a photo of him as a toddler. Many thought Warrington-born Jesse was too small to make it as a professional. But if there was one young man who came out of Manchester United's less-than-stellar season with his reputation enhanced, it was Lingard.

The theory went that with United's purchase of Alexis Sánchez, Lingard would lose his place and with that his chance of making the England starting line-up. But Jesse, loaned out to four different clubs in his earlier United days, dug in and showed his value. He credited manager José Mourinho for playing a major part in his journey to the finals, saying: 'He put that trust and faith in me to play me in big matches week-in, week-out.'

Jesse's brilliant goal against Panama showed his finishing ability was as good for his country as his club, and his link-up play with Dele Alli and Harry Kane was one of the key elements in England's success in the tournament. Lingard established himself as one of the big jokers in the England pack, and was encouraged by Southgate to enjoy himself. 'He wants us to have a mentality to play with freedom, play without fear, and that way we would enjoy our time more,' said Lingard.

Livewire Jesse is a positive influence on his team-mates. He told friends one of his greatest achievements was bringing the 'dab' dance craze into English football after Paul Pogba pioneered it at Juventus.

Lingard is close to his mum Kirsty, 49. After the win over Colombia, he posted a photo on Twitter, captioned: 'No mum, I'm not coming home.' Then a follow-up showed him hugging her in Russia, with the words: 'Because I said we ain't going home, she came here. Love you.' Kirsty is a former gymnast, and Jesse admits she was key to him making it at United and with England. Dad Roy George was born in England to parents from St Vincent in the Caribbean. Jesse's parents split soon after he was born but he stays in touch with his father, who used to play semi-professional football. He is also close to his younger siblings, Jasper and Daisy Boo.

JORDAN HENDERSON

MIDFIELDER

Age: 28

England caps: 44

England goals: 0

Club: Liverpool

Once accused by Sir Alex Ferguson of not being able to run properly, the Liverpool skipper covered every blade of grass in Russia. Many felt that Henderson deserved the captaincy ahead of Harry Kane after his season at Anfield, leading Jürgen Klopp's men to the Champions League Final. If the Sunderland-born star had any problems with Southgate's decision, though, they were not obvious as he held off the challenge of Eric Dier to take the role of midfield 'single pivot' in the England set-up.

Henderson was a teenage starlet for his hometown club and made his England debut at 20, although he did not feature for the Three Lions again until Frank Lampard's training-ground injury got him into Roy Hodgson's Euro 2012 squad from the standby list. Part of the squads that suffered pain and ridicule in 2014 and 2016, Henderson captained England six times under Southgate.

By nature a box-to-box midfielder, he put those instincts on hold to be the England fulcrum in Russia, picking up the pieces and making vital blocks and tackles. Henderson admitted that 'fellow Mackem' Jordan Pickford bailed him out following his shoot-out miss against Colombia, after receiving a blatant head-butt in the first half.

Jordan was born to Liz and Brian Henderson, and has one sister, Jody. He is married to Rebecca Burnett and has two children, three-year-old Alexa and Alba, one. Like all the players in the dynamic new England squad, he had solid family support, backed to the hilt by his fitness-teacher mum Liz and retired police-officer dad Brian. Brian knew a bit about the game – he used to play for Durham Police and, like his son, is a hardcore Sunderland fan.

HARRY KANE

FORWARD

Age: 24

England caps: 30

England goals: 19

Club: Tottenham Hotspur

Harry Kane has made the incredible journey from 'chubby' football reject to talismanic England captain and World Cup Golden Boot winner. He's the ultimate modern-day professional, with all the star qualities – dedication, discipline, determination and pure skill – to stay at the very top for years. But the most crucial ingredients are his love for football and the ability to battle back from bitter blows.

Born on 28 July 1993 in Walthamstow, east London, Harry went to Larkswood Primary School, then Chingford Foundation School – which England legend David Beckham had attended. 'Harry was clever, articulate and very humble,' said his English teacher, Denis McElligott, who also managed the school football team. 'If we were struggling, the tactic would be to give it to Harry – and he'd smash one in from the corner flag.'

From the age of six, Harry also played for Ridgeway Rovers, the same junior club as Becks. In fact, when Beckham launched a football academy in London in 2005, he invited along pupils from his old school – including 12-year-old Harry and his childhood sweetheart and future fiancée, Katie Goodland. The pair smiled shyly as they met the star and posed for pictures. That brush with Becks spurred football-mad Harry to work even harder.

Aged eight he had already suffered his first major blow – one from which many might never have recovered. He had been training with Arsenal but they let him go for being overweight. 'He was a bit chubby,' Gunners legend and then academy chief Liam Brady recalled. 'He wasn't very athletic, but we made a mistake.'

Harry remembers hearing the news: 'One day when I was eight, I was walking to the park with my dad, and he said right out of the blue, "I've got to tell you something." I said, "What is it?" Then he put his arm round my shoulder and said, "Well, Harry, Arsenal have released you. But don't worry. We'll work harder – and we'll find another club, all right?"' A trial with boyhood idols Tottenham Hotspur soon after came to nothing, too.

But in 2004, aged 11, persistence paid off and he joined Watford for a trial. Impressing in a match against Spurs, the north Londoners gave him another chance. This time he stayed and rose through Spurs' youth ranks. In January 2011, 17-year-old Harry was loaned to Leyton Orient, where he scored his first goal, against Sheffield Wednesday. More loan spells followed at Millwall, Norwich City and Leicester City.

He is still motivated today by the criticism from fans during those difficult days: 'He's just a one-season wonder'; 'Just a penalty merchant'; 'Good at tap-ins but nothing else'; 'Doesn't do it against the big clubs'.

At Leicester he struggled in the sidelines. 'I thought, "If I can't play for Leicester in the Championship, how am I supposed to play for Spurs in the Premier League?" That was the first time in my career that doubt crept in. My dad said, "Keep working – keep doing it and everything will be all right."' Of Arsenal's rejection Harry says: 'It was the best thing that ever happened to me. The first time we played them I had a chip on my shoulder. I was only eight when they let me go but every time we played them I thought, "All right, we'll see who's right and who's wrong."'

When Spurs appointed new manager Mauricio Pochettino in 2014, it all finally began to go right. The Argentinian – revered for his man-management – encouraged his chunky striker to lose the puppy fat. Determined Harry started to eat lean and clean. Now he only drinks during the close season. His body fat was 15 per cent when Poch arrived at White Hart Lane. Today it's 8 or 9 per cent – the perfect physical specimen. Poch, who spoke exclusively to *The Sun* during the World Cup, said: 'You need motivation in life, and Harry found it. The most important thing is that the person who made Harry Kane is Harry Kane.'

But Kane also recognises the role of his parents, Kim and Pat – who moved to London from Letterfrack, Co. Galway. 'I think the sporting genes come from Mum's side,' he said. 'Although Dad won't like me saying that. Her dad, Eric, was a good footballer and played at a decent level.' (Fortunately, Harry turned down Martin O'Neill's call to play for Ireland in 2014.) His parents guided him in other ways, too. Unlike

'YOU NEED MOTIVATION IN LIFE, AND HARRY FOUND IT. THE PERSON WHO MADE HARRY KANE IS HARRY KANE.'

MAURICIO POCHETTINO

hero Becks, Harry avoided tattoos: 'My dad always told me I would regret it when I was older.'

The setbacks helped Kane establish himself as a top player, respected by fellow Premier League pros. But Russia 2018 made him a global star. A powerful, influential presence during this mesmerising campaign, he is now regarded as one of the best out-and-out centre-forwards in the world. His six goals – two against Tunisia, three in the 6–1 Panama rout and one against Colombia – equalled Gary Lineker's Mexico haul in 1986.

Some saw Kane's pre-tournament declaration that he aimed to win the trophy *and* the Golden Boot – ahead of Lionel Messi and Cristiano Ronaldo – as a case of World Cup fever.

In fact, it showed his determination to set himself goals – and score them. But Kane – who had a spectacular season with Spurs and signed a new contract days before the World Cup – did much more. His tireless work off the ball, closing defenders and drawing free-kicks, showed his team ethic. Off the pitch, too, he never puts a foot wrong, setting an example to youngsters with his clean-cut image.

He lives with pregnant fiancée Katie and their one-year-old daughter Ivy in Essex. The couple got engaged last summer. 'We went to school together, so she's seen my whole career,' says Harry. 'Of course, she's finding it a little crazy now.' They have hired a chef at home to make sure his diet is right. His only vice is his mum's apple pie and custard – in moderation. The couple take their two Labradors, Brady and Wilson, for walks in parkland nearby, and Harry relaxes on the sofa watching NFL football, golf or his favourite TV show, *Dexter*.

England has been blessed with top-class centre-forwards over the years, but few were in a team young and talented enough to lose but go again. For Harry Kane, defeat to Croatia is one more blow he will use as motivation to come back stronger and better. And maybe, just maybe, lift the World Cup for England in 2022.

RAHEEM STERLING

MIDFIELDER/FORWARD

Age: 23

England caps: 43

England goals: 2

Club: Manchester City

10

It is fitting that Raheem Sterling grew up in the shadow of Wembley Stadium. He moved to London from Jamaica aged five and his road to Russia started when he played football in the area surrounding the iconic venue. The place where Geoff Hurst scored his hat-trick against West Germany, where Bobby Moore lifted the World Cup and where England's football team enjoyed their finest hour back in 1966.

'Football's Coming Home' was the chant from Three Lions' fans during their incredible journey in Russia, some 52 years later. And Raheem was a key player for Gareth Southgate as the team helped England fall back in love with football.

Russia 2018 was also a tournament where Sterling revealed a part of himself we had never seen before. Southgate wanted his players to tell their own stories and connect with the public after spending their club careers shielded from the spotlight. Sterling, through the forum of The Players' Tribune, spoke of his childhood, during which he helped his mother clean hotel rooms so she could pay for her education. 'I'll never forget waking up at five in the morning before school and helping her clean the toilets at the hotel in Stonebridge,' he wrote. 'I'd be arguing with my sister, like, "No! No! You got the toilets this time. I got the bed sheets."'

Football was Sterling's way out of his neighbourhood. It may be the home of football, but Wembley is a tough area. The stadium's famous arch 'was rising up over the top of the housing estates like a mountain,' says Sterling. In Russia there was touching footage of Sterling getting a call from his old coach and mentor Clive Ellington, who had a massive impact on getting him focused on football. They kept in touch and still banter with each other, despite Sterling establishing himself as one of the most valuable players in the Premier League.

His mother advised him to start at QPR, where he would get more of a chance to impress, compared with the big clubs in London such as Chelsea, Arsenal or Tottenham. She was right, too. He made such an impact as a teenager that Liverpool wanted to snap him up. Rafa

Benítez was the manager who brought him to Anfield, but it was under Brendan Rodgers that he shone in the first team. With Luis Suárez and Daniel Sturridge also part of the Kop attack, Liverpool almost won the Premier League.

They just missed out to Manchester City, who moved for Sterling a year later. At the time there were questions over whether £49 million was too much to pay for the forward, but he has proved to be a bargain ever since.

His relationship with England fans has not always been straight-forward. They booed him while he was in dispute over a new contract at Liverpool. At the disastrous Euro 2016 he called himself 'The Hated One' on social media after a draw with Russia.

Sterling, in some ways, was a victim of his own success. At club level his goal statistics have got better and better. Heading into the World Cup he scored 23 goals in all competitions during City's title-winning campaign. Before the tournament he had 38 caps – the equivalent of an entire Premier League season – but had only found the net twice, with his previous goal coming three years earlier.

Part of that can be explained by his different roles with club and country. For City, he plays as a wide forward and often gets on the end of crosses from pacy team-mates such as Leroy Sané. But Southgate used him in Russia as a support striker to Harry Kane, right through the middle and often as far forward as the England captain. So he got through plenty of work carrying the ball forward for the Three Lions, but not as many chances as he does with his club.

'He offers so much to the team,' said England team-mate Eric Dier. 'His willingness to make forward runs. Obviously, he's quality in possession. He can come short and link the play. He can make runs in behind. Off the ball his work rate is incredible. It's so clear to see, if you were to watch back all of our games, the importance he has to the team.'

Yet his position in the team was questioned. Southgate was not happy when he turned up a day late for duty on the eve of the tournament, with a mix-up over connecting flights to blame for him getting back to St George's Park. But the England manager kept faith in his talented forward and started him in the opening victory against Tunisia.

Again, Sterling's place appeared under threat after he missed a big early chance in Volgograd. Then later that week assistant boss Steve Holland was pictured with what looked like the team sheet for the match against Panama, which had Marcus Rashford replacing Sterling.

'OFF THE BALL HIS WORK RATE IS INCREDIBLE. IT'S SO CLEAR TO SEE, IF YOU WERE TO WATCH BACK ALL OF OUR GAMES, THE IMPORTANCE HE HAS TO THE TEAM.'

ERIC DIER

It turned out that the sheet was not the team selection – and it was Sterling who started in the thumping 6–1 win against England's Central American opponents.

Southgate continued to believe in him and the City star started to get credit for his hard work during matches, even if it was Kane getting the glory with the goals.

Back at England's ForRestMix hotel in Repino, Sterling was just one of the lads. On the first day he got to Russia he foolishly left his room unlocked, then returned to find five chairs and a plant waiting for him. He thinks he knows who the prankster was. He relaxed by watching *Money Heist*, a Spanish crime series on Netflix, then got to work on the training pitch, although he was the one joking around with his teammates and spraying them when the sprinklers were turned on.

It was a world away from where he grew up in Wembley. But he was at home on the biggest stage of them all – the World Cup.

JAMIE VARDY

FORWARD

Age: 31

England caps: 26

England goals: 7

Club: Leicester City

11

The biopic of Jamie Vardy's story has still not made it to the silver screen, but the real-life rags-to-riches tale is remarkable. Released by Sheffield Wednesday at 16, Vardy joined Stocksbridge Park Steels in football's eighth tier. While working as a technician making medical splints in 2007, a pub brawl saw him convicted of assault and made to wear an electronic tag for six months. He would play football in the tag and then have to be back indoors in Sheffield, rushing home after away matches, to maintain a night-time curfew.

Jamie was born James Richard Gill to dad Richard Gill, then aged 24, and mum Lisa Clewes, 18. He was an only child. His breakthrough as a player came in 2010 when former league side Halifax Town took a chance on him, and a year later he was at Fleetwood, scoring 31 goals in 36 Conference appearances. That form and his sheer pace caught the eye of Leicester, who paid £1 million to land him, but after a bright start, his form dropped off and Vardy even considered quitting. He rediscovered his knack for goals as Leicester were promoted, although the England call-up the following season was a surprise after just four Premier League goals.

Then came lift-off. Vardy was the cutting edge of the Foxes in the top tier, scoring in a record 11 straight league games as they stunned football by lifting the title in 2016. By May, everybody knew 'Jamie Vardy's having a party'. Jamie also scored against Wales at Euro 2016.

The striker married Rebekah in May 2016 and the couple have two children together. Jamie also has a third child, and is stepfather to two of Rebekah's children. Jamie and Rebekah's wedding, attended by showbiz stars including One Direction's Louis Tomlinson and rapper Tinchy Stryder, took place at Peckforton Castle in Cheshire.

KIERAN TRIPPIER

Kieran Trippier's stunning free-kick against Croatia was his first goal for his country – and made him only the third Englishman to score in a World Cup semi-final.

'Not bad for a Bury lad,' is how Kieran described his superb performances in Russia. And his home town's council agreed, awarding him the freedom of Bury for his achievement.

Although dubbed 'the Bury Beckham' for his dead-ball prowess, Trippier says his parents have kept him grounded while inspiring him to reach the very top. Dad Chris, a builder, and mum Eleanor, a supervisor at Costcutter, sacrificed time and money to help him when he joined the Manchester City youth ranks at the age of nine.

Kieran has three brothers, Chris, Curtis and Kelvin. His family are Manchester United fans but, despite being scouted by United when he was eight, he chose to join Manchester City's academy as he had friends there. Kieran is a dad himself now and loves family life. In June 2016 he married girlfriend Charlotte in Cyprus, and their first child, Jacob, was born in December later that year.

While he was at City, Kieran joined Burnley on loan, soon signing permanently for a nominal fee. Turf Moor was lift-off, and Trippier featured in the Championship team of the year for two seasons running, celebrating promotion under Sean Dyche in 2015. He never played for the Clarets in the top flight, though, instead making a £3.5-million move to Spurs, where Mauricio Pochettino used him as Kyle Walker's back-up. Following doubts over Walker's commitment to the club, Trippier was promoted over him for the end of the 2016–17 season. Walker's move to Manchester City cemented Trippier's position, although he still had to fight off competition from experienced summer recruit Serge Aurier.

RIGHT-BACK

Age: 27

England caps: 12

England goals: 1

Club: Tottenham Hotspur

12

JACK BUTLAND

GOALKEEPER

Age: 25

England caps: 8

England goals: 0

Club: Stoke City

13

Butland had long been tipped as the heir to Joe Hart's No. 1 shirt. He was in the squad for Euro 2012 and became the country's youngest ever senior keeper, aged 19 years and 158 days, against Italy in August the same year. But when Hart was dumped for this World Cup, it was Jordan Pickford who bagged the jersey.

Instead of coming as a blow to Butland, he was relieved to make the squad having spent the season fighting a losing relegation battle with Stoke, and playing his way back into contention after a serious ankle injury that kept him out of the game for 13 months. It was on England duty against Germany in Berlin in March 2016 that Butland suffered what felt like 'an explosion in my ankle'.

It could have finished his career, and he was later to phone his mum to tell her he might not play again. But he battled back and, along with Nick Pope, provided unwavering support to Pickford. He said: 'It's important that you're humble and respectful and you put all pride aside. Whoever gets selected can't succeed without the support and backing of the other two.'

Jack was born in Bristol and grew up in the genteel north Somerset town of Clevedon, the backdrop for scenes in TV drama *Broadchurch*. His family were rugby fans – his grandad and dad, Matt, played the game and he followed in their footsteps at Clevedon Community School. He once said his real claim to fame was that he got the better of England No. 8 Billy Vunipola in a Somerset Schools' Cup final.

Jack was discovered as a football prospect by Clevedon United, staying until he was 14, when he was signed by Birmingham City. He says the support of Matt and mum Jill were key to his development as a footballer. The goalie proposed to long-term girlfriend, air stewardess Annabel Peyton, in May 2018 while on a romantic holiday in Italy.

DANNY WELBECK

The Arsenal man probably had the toughest time of any of England's outfield players in Russia. Just a brief appearance off the bench in the 'dead' group game with Belgium, a match both sides were quite content to lose. But after the injury anguish of the last few years, Welbeck was pretty happy to know that Southgate wanted him in his squad.

He was born in Longsight, Manchester, and was spotted by boyhood club Manchester United as a six-year-old. Danny once said: 'I can't remember a time when I didn't kick a ball around. I grew up on a council estate three miles from Manchester city centre, and wanted to play every day, all day. I got spotted by Man U scouts, and by the time I was 14 I was playing for the under-18s.'

Russia was Welbeck's third tournament. He scored the winner against Sweden at Euro 2012 with a delightful heel-flick, and then did the hard work down the left in the first two games in Brazil in 2014. Welbeck's £16-million deadline-day move to Arsenal that September, as Radamel Falcao arrived at Old Trafford on loan, was bemoaned by those United fans who believed in the club's youth policy. He was determined to make his point, but the second of two serious knee injuries cost him a place at Euro 2016, after he had set England on their way to the finals with both goals against Switzerland in Basel in the opening qualifier.

A succession of injuries since then have hampered a player whose goal return of 16 from 40 England appearances is far from shabby. But Welbeck remains popular in the squad for his attitude, workrate and positive thinking.

Mum Elizabeth and dad Victor are both Ghanaian, and he has a brother, Chris. Welbeck's childhood hero was Thierry Henry. Danny once said, 'I just wanted to be doing the stuff he was doing. He was quality.'

FORWARD

Age: 27

England caps: 40

England goals: 16

Club: Arsenal

14

GARY CAHILL

CENTRE-BACK

Age: 32

England caps: 61

England goals: 5

Club: Chelsea

There was a point in the last season at which Gary Cahill could not get into the Chelsea team, and it did not bode well for his England prospects. Not only that, Southgate's preference for a more mobile back three as opposed to an orthodox back four meant Cahill was not going to be one of his first choices. It looked like the end of the line for him as an international, but he would not be pushed out of the picture altogether.

He fought his way back into the Chelsea team and captained the side to FA Cup success before departing for Russia. He had feared the worst, though, after being left out of the squad back in March, and Southgate joked that he had a little bet with himself that if he rang Cahill he would not pick up because he was expecting to be left out. Southgate revealed: 'I left Gary a voice message saying: "I don't only call when it's bad news."' Cahill, born to Janet and Hughie Cahill and raised in Dronfield, Derbyshire, admitted: 'I thought it would be bad news because you usually don't get a call if you're in the squad – you just get information sent to you about where to meet and at what time.'

As a teen Gary was scouted by clubs including Sheffield Wednesday, Barnsley and Derby County, but he decided to sign with Aston Villa. After three years at Bolton he was signed by Chelsea for £7 million in 2012. He was a boyhood Sheffield Wednesday supporter whose hero was Italia 90 star Des Walker. Gary said: 'I always wanted to be a footballer, like a lot of lads. Nothing else ever entered my head – if I hadn't made it, I'd be struggling.'

Until Cahill played for England, he was also eligible to play for the Republic of Ireland through an Irish grandparent. But his manager at Bolton and former Republic of Ireland international, Owen Coyle, said the player only ever wanted to represent England. Cahill's only start in Russia was in the Group G defeat against Belgium. With 61 England caps, he was the most experienced player in the World Cup squad.

15

PHIL JONES

When Phil Jones made his debut and breakthrough at Blackburn Rovers in 2010, marking Chelsea giant Didier Drogba out of the game, the accolades came quickly. Many, including Sir Alex Ferguson, saw Jones as 'the new Duncan Edwards', the brilliant Manchester United and England midfielder, one of the 'Busby Babes' lost in the Munich air disaster in 1958. Jones appeared to have everything – pace, anticipation, timing and bite.

Preston-born Phil attended St Paul's Primary School in the suburb of Farington Moss, where he is remembered for wanting to get out of class as quickly as possible so that he could play football in the park across the road. He was encouraged in the game by parents Mark, a firefighter and footballer who was on Preston's books as a schoolboy, and Helen, a full-time mum. Phil met wife-to-be Kaya Hall, a student, while playing for Blackburn. Kaya, who he married last year, gave birth to their daughter 10 days before the England team arrived in Russia.

Fergie was happy to pay £16.5 million to land the defender in 2011, when he was still a teenager. He once said of Jones, 'The way he is looking, he could be Manchester United's best ever player'. Seven years on, though, Jones has never quite fulfilled those early hopes, not helped by continuing uncertainty over what his best role is. He made his England debut as a right-back for Fabio Capello in 2011, but has played most of his matches as a centre-half and also took on Brazil in the Maracana in 2013 as a defensive midfielder.

Like so many members of the 'shadow' side in Russia, Jones played his part by ensuring he never let his head go down. He played in the 2–0 third-place play-off defeat to Belgium. Team spirit was, as Southgate agreed, absolutely crucial.

CENTRE-BACK

Age: 26

England caps: 26

England goals: 0

Club: Manchester United

16

FABIAN DELPH

MIDFIELDER

Age: 28

England caps: 15

England goals: 0

Club: Manchester City

Yorkshire lad Fabian had plenty to celebrate at this World Cup – England's historic run and the birth of his third daughter. The Manchester City star left the team hotel in Russia to fly home to wife Natalie when she went into labour. Fabian got a lift to Britain with the family of City team-mate Vincent Kompany on the Belgian's private jet straight after the group game defeat against Belgium. He returned to Russia in time for the Sweden match and described the whirlwind trip as 'amazing', joking that the shoot-out against Colombia, and Jordan Henderson's saved kick, hurried up the process. He said: 'I think it was the penalties that brought on the labour. I've got Hendo to thank for that.' Boss Gareth Southgate, who showed his human side by allowing Delph to fly home, quipped: 'Delphy is back with us, so he's thinking of asking Hendo to be the one that christens the kid.'

Delph was a surprise inclusion in the squad, especially as he was chosen as a midfielder despite having spent the season playing full-back for City. He did not figure at all in England's World Cup qualifying campaign, and had spent nearly two months on the sidelines between February and April with a muscle injury. His first Three Lions outing in two and a half years was the friendly against Nigeria on 2 June.

Midfield had always been his stock in trade, but he would be forgiven for having forgotten how to play there. Southgate, however, knew what he would get with Delph – honest, hard-working, no-nonsense commitment, together with adaptability and a touch of creativity thrown into the mix. He'd asked City boss Pep Guardiola about Delph a couple of weeks before the squad was announced and got the recommendation he needed.

He's a keen reader and told how he was inspired in Russia by superstar basketball trainer Tim Grover's book *Relentless: From Good to Great to Unstoppable*. Grover worked with legends Michael Jordan and Kobe Bryant, teaching them how to thrive under great pressure. Useful advice for an England World Cup star.

Delph was born and raised in a deprived area of Bradford by single mum Donna, along with two siblings. He has come a long way.

17

ASHLEY YOUNG

LEFT-BACK

Age: 33

England caps: 39

England goals: 7

Club: Manchester United

Ashley Young is proof that you are never too old to have a fresh start. Compared with the rest of the young lions, he is a veteran, the Manchester United full-back having played for England since 2007, with 39 caps and seven goals. He turned 33 two days before the semi-final against Croatia and impressed throughout the tournament.

Young made his first-team debut for Watford in the same month Trent Alexander-Arnold started at school. The Old Trafford man, a flying winger at Vicarage Road before a £9.65-million move to Aston Villa, looked to be heading for England lift-off under Fabio Capello. Key goals in crunch Euro 2012 qualifiers against Switzerland, Wales and Montenegro, either side of his £20-million move to United, were followed by the first goal of the Roy Hodgson era in Norway.

But Young, who was at school with F1 champ Lewis Hamilton, failed to sparkle in Ukraine at the Euro finals, missing his penalty in the last-eight shoot-out defeat to Italy, and he soon slipped out of the frame. Young took stick for 'diving' in United colours, but Gareth Southgate noted his reinvention as a full-back under José Mourinho and called him back into the squad.

With Danny Rose a fitness doubt and United club-mate Luke Shaw disappearing off the radar, Young earned a surprise England recall. The switch to three central defenders flanked by wing-backs made him a contender, although the March 2018 game with Italy was his first England start in almost five years. While his tendency to turn back inside onto his right foot did slow things up, that dead-ball delivery remained a key attribute and element in England's attacking armoury in Russia.

Young is married to Nicky Pike, his childhood sweetheart. They have two children, Tyler and Ellearna. He has three brothers – the younger two also play football. Lewis Young made his debut for Watford in 2008 and Kyle Young trained at the Arsenal academy.

18

MARCUS RASHFORD

On Manchester United's books since the age of seven, Rashford became an overnight sensation in 2016 when he scored two goals on his debut.

Marcus grew up in one of Manchester's toughest areas, the Northern Moor estate in Wythenshawe, where Channel 4's *Shameless* was filmed. Many of his peers ended up in gangs, but mum Mel, 54 – a devout Christian – kept him on the straight and narrow. She brought him up on her own with his siblings Chantelle, Dwaine, Claire and Dane.

In 2015, United moved him and the family into a £650,000 home in upmarket Sale. After that, Marcus started to soar, attending Ashton-on-Mersey School, a state academy sponsored by United, to study for a BTEC Diploma in Sport.

Marcus made the headlines after scoring twice in his first match, against Midtjylland in the Europa League, after Anthony Martial broke down in the warm-up. And when he followed that up with another double against Arsenal three days later, everybody stood up and took notice. Rashford finished those remarkable first few months an FA Cup winner, with an England debut goal – virtually his first touch in the shirt – and a place in the Euro 2016 squad.

It was clear, even from those first few months, that Rashford had it in him to be the real deal, although there were always going to be bumps along the way. There have been tough times; José Mourinho has always been the hardest of taskmasters and Rashford has not felt the love of the Special One at all times. Yet Southgate earmarked Rashford for a role in Russia, knowing his pace and strength could be a weapon for him to utilise. His goals against Liverpool at Old Trafford earlier in the season were further proof that the talent was there.

Marcus's girlfriend, Lucia Loi, who works in PR, was spotted in the stands when England were victorious over Colombia in the round of 16. A few days later, when England beat Sweden in the quarter-final, Rashford wept openly after the match. He tweeted a picture of himself wiping away tears, captioning it: 'Words can't describe . . . part of something special.'

England know there is more to come from The Rash in the future.

FORWARD

Age: 20

England caps: 25

England goals: 3

Club: Manchester United

19

DELE ALLI

MIDFIELDER

Age: 22

England caps: 30

England goals: 3

Club: Tottenham Hotspur

Abandoned by his father at the age of one week and brought up in difficult circumstances, Dele was unofficially adopted by the parents of MK Dons youth team-mate Harry Hickford when he was 13. By 16 he was making his debut for MK Dons, his first touch a back-heel against Cambridge City in the FA Cup, and soon Premier League scouts were making a bee-line for the city of concrete cows.

When a Dele-inspired Dons thrashed Louis van Gaal's United 4–0 in the League Cup there was even more interest, and it then became a question of when he would leave. A Liverpool fan and admirer of Steven Gerrard, Dele seemed destined for Anfield – but Spurs, encouraged by David Pleat, stumped up the cash to land him in 2015, although they let him see out the season in Buckinghamshire.

Since then, it has been a continual cycle of progression, goals for Spurs – the best of them an absolute stunner, flicking over his own head before volleying in, at Crystal Palace – and a brilliant strike against France on his full England debut. Club form has not wavered, despite some unfair suggestions that he was less productive last season than the one before. That ignored his change in role, having played effectively as Harry Kane's strike partner when Spurs were runners-up in 2016–2017, and then deeper last season.

Dele had a few questions to answer in Russia and was hampered by injury in the opener with Tunisia, but he came up with the goods against Sweden, scoring England's second goal.

Dele's girlfriend, the model Ruby Mae, jetted out to Russia to be with him and support him during the World Cup. He is an avid fan of the *Fortnite* video game, and often celebrates goals by copying the game's dance moves.

20

RUBEN LOFTUS-CHEEK

MIDFIELDER

Age: 20

England caps: 8

England goals: 0

Club: Chelsea

21

Ruben was born in Lewisham in south-east London, and was on Chelsea's books from the age of eight. Yet the midfielder has made fewer Premier League appearances for his own club than he has for Crystal Palace on loan last season. That, in truth, says more about Chelsea and their approach to young talent than about Loftus-Cheek, who could not have done more than he did at Selhurst Park.

Gareth Southgate was delighted when the youngster made that loan switch, as he hoped that a player he had identified, tracked and managed through England's junior ranks – Loftus-Cheek scored the winner in the final of the 2016 Toulon Tournament – would seize the opportunity and come good. And there can be no disputing that Southgate's hunch was proved right. Ex-Chelsea and England boss Glenn Hoddle once compared him to German legend Michael Ballack, saying: 'He reminds me of Ballack – physically and the way he plays. He gets in the box and he moves well off the ball'.

Loftus-Cheek was a surprise inclusion in the squad for the November friendlies, but he grabbed his chance with both hands in a 90-minute appearance against Germany that answered plenty of questions. Any remaining ones were dismissed by the way he coped with the pressures of being in a World Cup squad.

Ruben's mum Juliette Cheek is British and his father Trevor Loftus is Guyanese. Ruben is also the half-brother of former Newcastle striker Carl Cort and ex-Crystal Palace defender Leon Cort.

Brave on the ball, calm in possession, Loftus-Cheek is going places. The World Cup can only crank up the speed at which he gets there.

TRENT ALEXANDER-ARNOLD

RIGHT-BACK

Age: 19

England caps: 2

England goals: 0

Club: Liverpool

22

Sir Alex Ferguson once asked a young Alexander-Arnold why he hadn't tried to join Manchester United. The youngster told him it was because 'Mum doesn't drive on motorways'. His gran Doreen Carling was Sir Alex's first girlfriend when the couple dated as teens in Glasgow.

The youngest member of the England squad at 19, Trent played in Liverpool's Champions League Final defeat against Real Madrid, in which you would never have known he was so young, after the team's brilliant run to Kiev. Then he found himself part of England's magic carpet ride in Russia.

He was always going to be a squad member rather than a starter in this World Cup, but arguably he was the one player who made a genuine case for inclusion in the final group game against Belgium, even if Kieran Trippier's stand-out displays meant that the Tottenham player was nailed on to come straight back in.

Elder brother Tyler acts as Trent's agent and chief cheerleader. Younger brother Marcel loves to watch the defender in action, too. 'Both of them are so supportive in their different ways,' Trent has said. Mum Dianne, 51, has been his rock, backing him every step of the way. Trent is also the nephew of former Reading and Millwall player John Alexander. Trent still lives at home with Dianne and businessman dad Michael Arnold, 56, and has no desire to leave just yet.

Trent is an ambassador for An Hour for Others, a Liverpool-based charity that provides food and cooking lessons to underprivileged members of the community.

The teenager – a graduate from the Liverpool academy, having been born and raised in the city and first spotted as a six-year-old – has the potential to be a 100-capper. Steven Gerrard was among the first to spot his potential, and such has been his rise over the past 12 months that Nathaniel Clyne, England's first-choice right-back a couple of years ago, may well have to move clubs to get regular football.

NICK POPE

Being the third-choice goalkeeper means you travel to a tournament knowing you are probably just along for the ride. But Pope, whose first taste of Premier League football arrived only when he replaced the crocked Tom Heaton for Burnley against Crystal Palace in September 2017, went through every training-ground drill with the England squad as if he were the starter.

Back in 2011 Pope was poised to start studying for a degree at Nottingham University. Then Charlton Athletic came knocking, plucking him from non-league Bury Town. But Soham-born Nick stood his ground about the importance of education and the Addicks agreed that he could continue to study *and* play. They also decided he was such a good prospect at 19 that they agreed to fund him on a degree course in sports science at Roehampton. Nick said at the time: 'I'd already planned to go to university, so I'm certain it will benefit me in the future, and the club are paying my fees, which definitely helps.' This showed the strong will and intelligent nature of the boy who replaced Heaton, England's No. 3 before he took the jersey, at Premier League Burnley.

The goalkeeper has always been a grafter. When he was released by Ipswich at 16, he did a milk round and worked at Next to earn a few bob while studying at West Suffolk College and playing for Bury Town reserves. Charlton came calling but Pope spent four years on loan at non-leaguers Harrow, Welling, Cambridge and Aldershot, as well as spells with York and Bury in League Two, before finally getting his chance at The Valley.

Promoted Burnley paid £1.3 million to land him in 2016, but he spent most of his first season as third choice behind Heaton and Paul Robinson. Former England No. 1 Robinson's retirement opened the door, and Pope capitalised on Heaton's misfortune to walk through it and into Southgate's squad after conceding just 35 goals in as many appearances.

Off the pitch, Nick has been going steady with girlfriend Shannon Horlock, 23, the daughter of former Manchester City tough-guy midfielder Kevin Horlock, for several years.

GOALKEEPER

Age: 26

England caps: 1

England goals: 0

Club: Burnley

23

MEANWHILE...
TOURNAMENT BUILD-UP

Summer started with toned, gorgeous singletons being the topic of conversation – who had coupled up and who had been mugged off. Yes, *Love Island* was back on TV and threatening to upstage the World Cup in many households.

England were barely on the bookies' radar and 'It's Coming Home' was just an ironic chant after our embarrassing exit from the Euros against Iceland. What had recently happened in Salisbury had left fans fearful of flying out to Russia, as memories of the Skripals' poisoning were still fresh. The UK had blamed Russia for the attack, and Prime Minister Theresa May would not be flying out to support the Three Lions. And nor would FA president Prince William. Relations between Russia and England were at an all-time low.

But as the heatwave cranked up, so did the Russian charm offensive. Russian train conductors were given lessons in how to smile, violent fans were banned from attending the games and Will Smith was roped in to perform on the official anthem. As *Love Island* had its first evictions, the public slowly started talking about some different toned hunks – 23 of them. More than a million people were expected to travel to Russia for the month-long tournament – only a few thousand of them being England fans – and an estimated three billion would watch on television.

>>>>

The tournament went off with a bang, thanks to a surprising performance from Robbie Williams singing 'Let Me Entertain You' at the opening ceremony. At one point, Robbie – resplendent in a red leopard-print suit – angered international audiences by flipping his middle finger up and pointing it directly at the camera. Some interpreted it as an impromptu protest at Russia's anti-gay policies, but the singer later said it was intended as a one-minute countdown to the first match, Russia versus Saudi Arabia.

As for the football, England weren't expected to get a look in – even though big guns Italy and the Netherlands had failed to qualify. Germany were the defending champions, still riding high after their astonishing 7–1 defeat of Brazil in the last World Cup. They had won all 10 of their qualifying games, scoring an impressive 43 goals and only conceding four. Pundits pointed towards Brazil as potential champs, having won the tournament five times and coming to Russia with a strong squad that included superstar Neymar, Philippe Coutinho and Paulinho. Spain, once all-conquering, had suffered blow after blow in recent tournaments, crashing out in the group stages in 2014 and knocked out in the round of 16 at Euro 2016. But the team had breezed through the qualifying rounds, with nine wins and one draw.

Other teams had standout players who could see them take home the World Cup – Argentina had Messi, Uruguay had Suárez, and Euro 2016 champs Portugal had Ronaldo. And Russia, although the lowest-ranked team in the tournament, did have home advantage in a nation of 144 million. France had built a spectacular squad with a wealth of talent – in Griezmann, Mbappé, Kanté and Pogba they had the players that could take them all the way. Belgium were seen as 'dark horse' outsiders, thanks to a talented team that included Hazard, De Bruyne and Lukaku.

England's young lions, shepherded by Gareth Southgate for the first time, had quietly roared through the qualifying rounds and comfortably won their group. But expectations remained low. As the heatwave settled in and Britain was treated to a summer the likes of which we hadn't seen since 1976, England fans poured into pub beer gardens, coaxed out by the sunshine to swap *Love Island* for football. The 2018 World Cup was under way, but Southgate's 23-man squad weren't expected to get very far.

How wrong we all were.

IN THE

In the sleepy Russian town of Repino – population 2,400 – there was little to suggest the world's biggest football tournament was about to explode an hour away in St Petersburg. The little shop near England's hotel sold no World Cup souvenirs. And unlike so many pubs in England, there was no bunting decorating the cafes and supermarket.

England arrived at their coastal base camp more in hope than expectation. But the young squad's body language as they stepped out of the bus at the ForRestMix Club seemed upbeat. Camouflage-clad military police were stationed outside the health spa, set in a birch and pine forest, and cops regularly patrolled the quiet streets around the grounds.

Yet inside, Gareth Southgate was creating a happy camp. The blockbuster video game *Fortnite* has 40 million fans around the globe – including many of the England squad. The Three Lions revealed they bonded by teaming up to play the survival game. Dele Alli was the self-proclaimed king of the dressing room. The game features a world in which a freak storm has wiped out 98 per cent of the Earth's population, leaving the rest to fight each other to the death. Although *Fortnite* relaxed and unified the squad, there was a competitive edge. Spurs midfielder Alli said: 'It's good fun, we just have

some banter. It's a great way to wind down. I'm going away with 22 of my brothers, so we all get on well. We've brought [*Fortnite*] here. I play and I'm better than Eric [Dier]! I have to say I'm the best in the England squad. Just now we played – me, Harry Kane, John Stones and Jamie Vardy against Harry Maguire, Nick Pope, Kyle Walker and Kieran Trippier. It was the first to three wins, and my team won.'

Some of the squad relaxed by playing the card game Uno. Kane confessed that others planned to watch TV reality show *Love Island*, which was getting impressive viewing figures in the UK. He said: 'Not me personally but some of the lads have been talking about it. If we can actually get it in Russia, some of them will be following it closely.' Ashley Young's room became the *Love Island* viewing area.

When their football careers finish, a few of the team could get jobs as baristas; the hotel had a high-spec

professional coffee machine, so rather than queue up to order a cappuccino, the players learned to make their own from scratch.

A media centre was set up at a nearby hotel, where players would talk to the press while taking them on at darts, pool or ten-pin bowling. It was in stark contrast to previous tournaments, where players were wrapped up in cotton wool and discouraged from speaking to the media.

Belgium – with a host of Premier League stars including Manchester United's Romelu Lukaku, Chelsea's Eden Hazard and Kevin De Bruyne of Manchester City – were Group G favourites. Many predicted England would do well to outsmart Tunisia, who were 21st in the FIFA rankings, nine below England. The Three Lions hadn't won the opening game of a major tournament since they beat Paraguay in the 2006 World Cup. That needed to be fixed.

ENGLAND CAMP

GROUP G | MATCH 1

MONDAY
18
JUNE

Tunisia 1–2 England

Sassi 35 (pen.)   Kane 11
                                   Kane 90+1

Gareth Southgate praised England for holding their nerve after Harry Kane's dramatic late goal got the Three Lions' campaign off to a winning start in Volgograd. England hadn't won their opening game at a major tournament for twelve years, and they looked set to pay the price for wasting a host of chances until captain Kane rescued them. The Tottenham striker had given England the lead after 11 minutes, only for Tunisia to draw level ten minutes before half-time when Kyle Walker conceded a soft penalty. With chances at a premium in the second half, a draw seemed inevitable. But a minute into added time, Kane popped up with a cool close-range header after Harry Maguire flicked on Kieran Trippier's corner.

Coach Southgate, who celebrated on the pitch at the end with a double fist pump, said: 'We played exciting football and created so many clear-cut chances, especially in the first half, and were in total control in the second half. Good teams score late goals. We have talked about this for a long time – that we want to be a team that score late goals. I was most proud of the way we kept playing, even though the clock was running down. We stayed patient and didn't just throw the ball in the box. If we had drawn, even though it would have made life more difficult for us, I would have been proud of the performance. We recovered well from a really harsh decision and kept our composure. At 1–1, we had a plan: to keep probing, but don't get caught on the counter-attack. At the end, the pressure built and built. We did the right things and made good decisions and were good value for the win. Remember, we're a team who are improving and developing. There will always be things we can get better at. We're a long way from perfection.'

England began at breakneck speed and should have had it won in the opening half hour. Jesse Lingard almost provided the dream start when Dele Alli set him up, but his low shot was superbly saved with his foot by keeper Mouez Hassen. From the resulting corner, Hassen kept out Maguire's header. Two minutes later, Alli fed Lingard on the left and his low ball across the box found Sterling at the far post, but the Manchester City forward somehow screwed the ball wide. A late offside flag spared his blushes.

England were threatening to overwhelm Tunisia and took a deserved lead after 11 minutes. Kane's deflected shot went off for a corner, Ashley Young took the set-piece and John Stones powered a header towards the top corner. Hassen clawed it off the line but Kane was on hand to tuck in the rebound. Tunisia suffered another setback when their keeper left the pitch in tears after suffering a shoulder injury, to be replaced by Farouk Ben Mustapha. The chances kept coming. Jordan Henderson tested Ben Mustapha with a volley, Lingard shot wide from a Young cross and a Maguire header from a Trippier free-kick was saved by the substitute keeper.

Tunisia had rarely threatened, but England were stunned after 33 minutes when referee Wilmar Roldán awarded the Carthage Eagles a penalty. As a harmless-looking cross floated across the box, Kyle Walker caught Fakhreddine Ben Youssef with a flailing arm and the Colombian official pointed to the spot. There was a two-minute delay as the referee waited for confirmation from the VAR team that he didn't need to review the decision. Walker was yellow-carded and, although keeper Jordan Pickford dived the right way, Ferjani Sassi tucked the ball just inside the post.

The goal seemed briefly to knock England's confidence, and to add to Southgate's worries, Dele Alli appeared to be struggling with a thigh injury. However, it wasn't long before the Three Lions came close again. After 39 minutes, a Young free-kick to the far post was met by Maguire. His header dropped to Alli, whose back-header looped over

'WE PLAYED EXCITING FOOTBALL AND CREATED SO MANY CLEAR-CUT CHANCES, ESPECIALLY IN THE FIRST HALF, AND WERE IN TOTAL CONTROL IN THE SECOND HALF. GOOD TEAMS SCORE LATE GOALS.'

GARETH SOUTHGATE

the keeper on to the crossbar before being hacked off the line. The loose ball fell invitingly to Stones but he miscued his shot. Amid the chaos, Kane was wrestled to the ground, but the referee ignored England's penalty appeals.

Another set-piece, this time a Trippier free-kick, caused more mayhem, but Lingard's shot was deflected over. Then Trippier's superb pass set Lingard clear. The Manchester United midfielder beat keeper Ben Mustapha to the ball, but his toe-poke rolled agonisingly onto the foot of the post.

At the start of the second half, it wasn't long before England – with Alli surprisingly still on the pitch despite his injury – were threatening again. After 51 minutes they won another corner and Kane was clearly bundled over, but referee Roldan failed to award a penalty and, to England's dismay, there was no suggestion from the VAR team for him to review it. Tunisia, who hadn't won a World Cup finals game in 11 attempts since winning the first match of their debut appearance in 1978, were happy to settle for a point. England dominated possession but struggled to create chances. The closest they came was a Trippier free-kick that drifted wide.

Southgate made his first change after 68 minutes, sending on Marcus Rashford for Sterling, while Alli made way for Ruben Loftus-Cheek with ten minutes left. Loftus-Cheek, in particular, gave England fresh impetus and, after 88 minutes, he combined with Trippier on the right and cut back inside to roll the ball across the box for Rashford. However, rather than shooting, Rashford let the ball run for Lingard, who was unable to get a shot away.

Despite England's near-total dominance, a draw seemed inevitable as the fourth official raised the board indicating there would be four minutes of added time. However, a minute into injury time, Loftus-Cheek's persistence earned the Three Lions another corner, and when Trippier swung it over, Maguire got his head to the ball and, as it squirted to the far post, the unmarked Kane was there to guide a header just inside the post. The ecstatic captain raced away to the corner, where he was buried under a sea of bodies as England celebrated wildly.

There was no doubt the victory was deserved. Tunisia's penalty was their only shot on target, compared with England's eight. In total, the Three Lions had 18 attempts on goal. Kane's goals were his first at a major tournament after flopping at the 2015 European Under-21 Championship and Euro 2016. His double made him the first England player to score twice in a World Cup finals match since Gary Lineker against Cameroon at Italia 90.

Southgate said: 'Harry is a top striker. I'm delighted for him, as we would be asking questions about him not scoring in tournament football if he

'IT'S A MASSIVE BOOST FOR US. WE ALWAYS SAID WE WOULD KEEP GOING AND FIGHTING.'

JORDAN HENDERSON

hadn't scored tonight. I'm pleased for him, but I know that for him it will be more important that the team has won a game in the World Cup.'

Kane, who admitted he struggled to cope with the swarms of midges in the hot and humid conditions in Volgograd, said: 'I'm absolutely buzzing! It's what dreams are made of. It's such a good feeling. Obviously you get such a good feeling, any goal you score, but to score a winner in the World Cup like that is just incredible. There are always a bit of nerves, a bit of excitement, but we got into the game very quickly. We could have scored two or three and put the game to bed. It went to 1–1 and the momentum changed a bit. It's always in the back of your mind that it isn't going to be your day, but that's why you work for 90-plus minutes.' Of the midges, Kane said: 'We got told there would be a lot of flies and when we went out for the match it was a lot more than we thought. We all had bug spray on. Some of them went in your eyes, some in your mouth, but it is about dealing with what comes your way.'

Southgate and Kane were both miffed at the referee failing to award at least two penalties for fouls on Kane at set-pieces and wondered why VAR wasn't used. Kane claimed: 'We could have had a couple of penalties, especially when you look at theirs. At a few corners they were trying to grab, hold and stop us running. That's what VAR is there for. Maybe it was a bit of justice to score at the back post at the end.' Southgate said: 'If it's a penalty at one end it has to be a penalty at the other. We have to leave it to the powers that be, but it's clear that if a foul is given against Kyle Walker, then it has to be given for Harry Kane being hauled to the ground.'

Although the Tunisian penalty appeared harsh, Walker admitted: 'It's one of those things that I'm going to have to take on the chin. I've got my arms up. I think I did catch him. In the Premier League, probably not. In the World Cup, it might be. It's a learning curve for me. Next time, I'll head it away and ask questions afterwards.'

Liverpool star Henderson, given the nod ahead of Eric Dier in midfield, was one of England's stand-out performers. He said: 'It's a massive boost for us. We always said we would keep going and fighting. Thankfully that paid off for us tonight with a big goal and a big win. Maybe we were thinking about the chances we missed. You can't do that in a World Cup. The second half we kept going, but we didn't keep creating chances. They defended deeper, but we got the goal in the end.'

Tunisia coach Nabil Maaloul said: 'Kane is one of the best attackers in the Premier League and that is why he is highly sought-after by the highest clubs. I think he was behind the victory. It was him who was always there at the right time.'

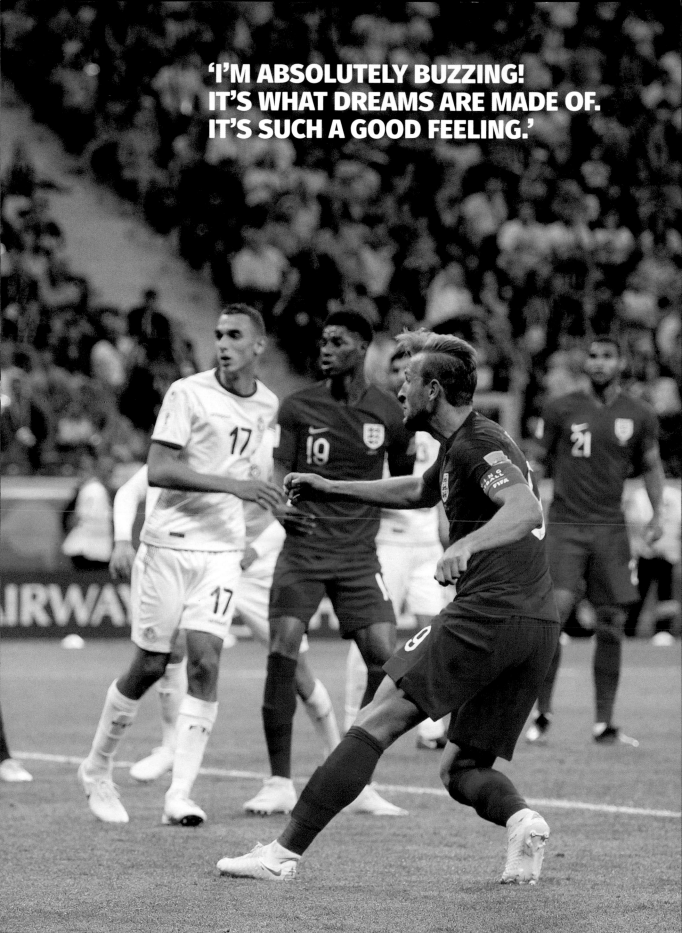

'I'M ABSOLUTELY BUZZING!
IT'S WHAT DREAMS ARE MADE OF.
IT'S SUCH A GOOD FEELING.'

TUNISIA V ENGLAND

ROAROMETER: 80 dB – noisy dishwasher

FOOTBALL TO HOME:
2,425 miles (3,903 km)

V

Two years since England's disastrous defeat to Iceland in Euro 2016, 21 million of us tuned in to watch the agony begin again… Yet for once England got it right – a solid attacking performance by a young, fresh team ended in victory thanks to two-goal Harry Kane. Mauricio Pochettino, his Argentinian boss at Spurs, said: 'I'm so proud. When he scored in the last minute I was running around like an England fan.'

Richard Wilson, 57, from Teddington, West London, said: 'We're virtually assured of qualifying for the knockout stage already and can start believing.'

The midges in the stadium were more dangerous than Tunisia's attack – fans were plagued by the little blighters. Patrick Vockins, 26 – one of 2,100 travelling England supporters – said: 'We were attacked by clouds of tiny flies. They get everywhere.'

Back home, celebrations were more muted. One fan fell through the roof of a bus shelter. But joy across the country was tempered by the knowledge that it could all still go wrong. Crowds in pubs might have sung 'Football's Coming Home', but not many really believed it. And most made it to work the following day.

Ironic comic Sathnam Sangera captured the mood:
'Two actual shots on goal. We're gonna win the World Cup!'

LION CUBS

These were the England lion cubs who roared on the world stage in Russia. Just like millions of youngsters, they once dreamed of glory on scuffed turf, shooting goals between jumpers in the back yard and training in the biting rain. As they grew in size and confidence, these young men went from being their families' pride to the pride of a nation. But how much have they really changed? Can you identify the players from these photos of their younger selves?

Living up to his name, this starter was aged just four here.

Flash dresser showed lots of selfie-control in England's midfield.

This stylish defender was always head and shoulders above the rest.

Isn't he glovely? England's number one pick.

His currency has grown thanks to surging runs.

6

A change in position was a stroll for this star born with Sheffield steel.

7

England's rock in defence started out as a Barnsley youth.

8

Once told he was too small to make it as a professional, this player was a huge figure in Russia.

9

England ex-Becks: never mind Goldenballs, here's Goldenboot and his wife-to-be.

10

Give him a big Hend! One day waistcoats will come back into fashion.

11

It's been a long journey from Man City reject to World Cup scorer.

England's fairytale World Cup start required a fairytale recovery day – so they cooled off in the pool on inflatable unicorns. The buoyant squad arrived back at their Repino HQ at 6am after taking an overnight flight from Volgograd to St Petersburg. Later they played basketball and took part in a stretching session at the gym. Those who didn't start the game had a full day of training.

With a precious first victory under their belts, the mood in the camp was buzzing even more than the midges that had plagued the Volgograd pitch. Pictures of the squad training showed beaming smiles, close camaraderie and a side relishing the next Group G match. Victory over Panama would see England qualify for the last 16 with a game to spare.

Back home, there was a frenzy of speculation about who would be in the starting XI. Assistant manager Steve Holland was pictured holding training notes that suggested Raheem Sterling would be dropped in favour of Marcus Rashford, who had come on as sub to replace Sterling against Tunisia. The pictures, which also indicated Ruben Loftus-Cheek would replace the injured Dele Alli, sparked debate among England fans.

But Jordan Henderson was quick to defend Sterling. He said: 'I don't think there should be any noise about his performance the other night. I looked at what he brings to England, with his pace to run in behind and drop in and link the play. He was phenomenal for City last season; everyone needs to get behind him.'

Holland said sorry to the squad for letting slip the possible team. According to Kyle Walker: 'He gave his apologies and said it was the first time he had messed up in 20 years, which we had a bit of a laugh about because his refereeing skills are not great.'

Harry Maguire joked that England's formidable Yorkshire contingent would be up for a scrap against Panama. Maguire, John Stones, Kyle Walker, Danny Rose, Fabian Delph and Jamie Vardy all hail from the White Rose county. Harry said: 'There's a lot of Yorkshire lads in the squad and they tend to be defenders or defensive midfielders. It must be something from the culture or the area. We work hard in the gym, we work hard on set-plays. And if Panama want to be physical, we will be prepared. I've had a broken nose and a few black eyes. It's part and parcel of the game. As long as we come off victorious I'll be smiling.'

England boss Gareth Southgate decided not to train the lads in scorching conditions in Nizhny Novgorod the day before the Panama match. Instead, they enjoyed a well-deserved day off with their families, relaxing in the Russian sunshine. The medical team had a busier day than expected, though, after Southgate dislocated his right shoulder while jogging. His arm was in a sling for the England team meeting, and he joked that he had been on for a record 10k time.

Southgate told his players to 'create their own history'. He added: 'They're a young team who will get better and better. I'm intrigued to find out how far they can go.' It turned out to be very far indeed.

SUNDAY
24
JUNE

England 6–1 Panama

Stones 8	Baloy 78
Kane 22 (pen.)	
Lingard 36	
Stones 40	
Kane 45+1 (pen.)	
Kane 62	

Harry Kane dared England fans to believe after the Three Lions ripped up the record books with a stunning six-goal demolition of Panama. England booked their place in the last 16 with a game to spare, thanks to their biggest win at a World Cup.

Captain Kane led the way in Nizhny Novgorod with a hat-trick, making him only the third England player to net a treble at the World Cup after Geoff Hurst in the 1966 final against West Germany and Gary Lineker against Poland in 1986. Kane said: 'We're not getting too ahead of ourselves. We've got to keep it going, but yes, you have to believe. If you want to achieve anything in life, you have to believe.'

His two penalties and a lucky deflection took his tally to five in two games. That put him on top in the race for the Golden Boot, and he said: 'There's going to be a lot of talk about it, but it's about the wins. Hopefully I can score more goals and help my team.'

Panama couldn't cope with England's pace and power, with three of the goals coming from set-pieces. Kane added: 'It could have been a tough game, but we started well. We've been working hard on set-pieces and they came together today. We've got to enjoy this. It's not every year that we go through after two games.'

England's free-kick and corner routines caused panic in the Central Americans' defence, and they resorted to tactics more at home in a WWE ring than on a football field. After the controversy over Tunisia not being penalised in the opening game, Egyptian referee Gehad Grisha was on red alert for similar incidents. Kane said: 'We knew it would be an aggressive game, that they would do everything to stop us. I thought the discipline was really good from us. We didn't get involved in anything silly. We made sure the ref was aware of the holding and pulling, and we got what we deserved.'

The England captain kept his cool to smash home the first penalty after the Panama players' attempts to unsettle him. He produced another emphatic strike with his second spot-kick, and then inadvertently diverted a Ruben Loftus-Cheek shot into the net for his hat-trick. He said: 'I have a routine for penalties. For the first penalty, I think I put the ball down about three times. It was about going through the same routine, picking a corner and sticking with it. The third goal was one of the luckiest goals of my career, but I'll take it! As a striker, sometimes you go through spells when you're scoring and other times it's not so good. It's been going my way, so hopefully that will continue.'

Belgium had laid down a marker in Group G the previous day when they booked their place in the last 16 by following up their 3–0 win over Panama by thrashing Tunisia 5–2. But England finished the day on top of the group because their victory left the nations with identical records for wins, goal difference and goals scored – putting England top by virtue of having received one less yellow card.

The Belgians had struggled to overcome Panama, but England had the game won by half-time after romping into a 5–0 lead. It was actually Panama who had the first two chances after a sloppy start by England. Édgar Bárcenas blazed over from distance and then set up Aníbal Godoy for an even better opportunity, but he sliced his shot wide. However, if England fans watching in the Sunday lunchtime sunshine at home were worried a disaster was about to unfold, they were soon pinching themselves as England tore the World Cup debutants to shreds.

As against Tunisia, it was a set-piece that did the damage, John Stones thumping a header past keeper Jaime Penedo from a Kieran Trippier corner after eight minutes. England would have had a case for a penalty had Stones not scored, with Harry Maguire being bundled over. Bárcenas went close with a curling shot as Panama tried to respond, but it was 2–0 after 22 minutes when Jesse Lingard was pushed over by Fidel Escobar as he bore down on goal. There was a two-minute delay as Panama protested, but Kane kept his composure to rifle the ball into the top corner.

Lingard was coming in for some rough treatment, but there was no stopping him when, after 36 minutes, he played a one–two with Raheem Sterling and curled a stunning shot into the top corner. Just four minutes later, it was 4–0 and Stones was the scorer again – meaning he now had more World Cup finals goals than England's record goalscorer, Wayne Rooney. The goal came from a well-rehearsed free-kick routine, Trippier rolling the ball short to Jordan Henderson on the edge of the box and the Liverpool man chipping the ball to the far post for Kane to head it back across goal to Sterling. The Manchester City forward's close-range header was saved, but Stones followed up to head the ball in.

This was the first time England had scored four goals in a World Cup match since the 1966 final and, just before half-time, Gareth Southgate's men went one better when Kane scored his second penalty. Godoy wrestled the England captain to the ground at a corner and Kane produced a carbon-copy penalty into the top corner.

England were now assured of winning their first two matches at a World Cup for the first time since 2006 and had already outstripped the nation's previous biggest World Cup wins – 3–0 versus Denmark in 2002, and against both Poland and Paraguay in 1986. But they went into the second half knowing a six-goal winning margin would put

'I THOUGHT THE DISCIPLINE WAS REALLY GOOD FROM US. WE DIDN'T GET INVOLVED IN ANYTHING SILLY. WE MADE SURE THE REF WAS AWARE OF THE HOLDING AND PULLING, AND WE GOT WHAT WE DESERVED.'

HARRY KANE

them top of Group G on goal difference.

The second half was relatively subdued, but the sixth goal did come after 62 minutes when a sequence of 25 consecutive passes ended with Loftus-Cheek – starting in place of the injured Dele Alli – trying his luck from distance, the ball hitting Kane's heel and flying in. That meant England had scored as many goals in one game as they had in their previous seven World Cup matches combined.

Southgate was able to take off Kane and Lingard shortly afterwards and give Jamie Vardy and Fabian Delph a taste of the action. But, as England took their foot off the gas, Panama grabbed a consolation goal with 12 minutes left. They had already spurned a couple of half chances before some sloppy defending from a free-kick allowed sub Felipe Baloy to slide the ball past Jordan Pickford.

That was the last meaningful action as the match petered out, and when the final whistle blew, Southgate again celebrated with a double fist pump, showing no signs of discomfort after dislocating his shoulder while out running in the build-up to the match.

However, despite the record win, Southgate admitted: 'I didn't particularly like the performance. I didn't like the start and I didn't like their goal at the end. I guess the bits in the middle were pretty good. I'm being hyper-critical. The second half is very difficult, no matter what you say to the players at half-time, at 5–0 up. We talked about the importance of one more goal to be top of the group, which is why the goal at the end is so disappointing. It's strange, because I enjoyed the win against Tunisia more. We probably at times played better the other day but today we were better in front of goal. I know how many people were watching at home, and it's great to give them something to cheer about. Confidence-wise, it was important for the lads to know that they can score goals and for Jesse Lingard especially. And it was great for the captain to get a hat-trick so he didn't get the hump when I brought him off! I'm really pleased with the ruthless nature of the first half. Once we opened the scoring we really started to look a threat. There were a couple of really special moves in that first half, in particular. We also continue to be a real threat from our set-plays.'

Commenting on England keeping their discipline despite Panama's rough-house tactics, Southgate added: 'We knew that was likely to happen. I was pleased the referee was strong. More importantly, we didn't react to it.' He went on to hail captain Kane: 'We wouldn't swap him for anyone at the tournament in terms of number nines. He has started brilliantly. He's there in the scoring charts, up at the top.' And asked if it would be better to lose to Belgium to avoid a potential

'I KNOW HOW MANY PEOPLE WERE WATCHING AT HOME, AND IT'S GREAT TO GIVE THEM SOMETHING TO CHEER ABOUT. CONFIDENCE-WISE, IT WAS IMPORTANT FOR THE LADS TO KNOW THAT THEY CAN SCORE GOALS.'

GARETH SOUTHGATE

meeting with Brazil in the quarter finals, the England manager said: 'I've heard talk of it being better finishing second, but I think that's dangerous territory.'

Two-goal hero Stones said: 'To score my first goals for England was something special, especially at a World Cup. It's not something I thought I would do at the start of the day,' while fellow scorer Jesse Lingard said: 'It's an amazing feeling. There's a great team spirit at the moment.'

Panama coach Hernán Darío Gómez admitted: 'Panama are a small young child in football. We were feeling rather frightened at half-time. What we did was try to avoid a bigger catastrophe. England are totally spectacular – a beautiful team.' Gómez approached Southgate before the second half and he revealed: 'I told him, "We're going to play cool and calm now." I tried during half-time to tell my players to be more composed, to play in an orderly fashion.'

'WE'RE NOT GETTING TOO AHEAD OF OURSELVES.
WE'VE GOT TO KEEP IT GOING, BUT YES, YOU HAVE
TO BELIEVE. IF YOU WANT TO ACHIEVE ANYTHING
IN LIFE, YOU HAVE TO BELIEVE.'

HARRY KANE

ENGLAND V PANAMA

ROAROMETER: 120 dB – Thunderclap

FOOTBALL TO HOME:
2,101 miles (3,382 km)

V

 @GaryLineker

This is getting silly. Last time England scored 4 or more goals in a World Cup was the 1966 WC final.

Victory would virtually assure England a place in the knockout stages – and after the Canaleros' 3–0 loss to Belgium, our optimism grew. But who could have predicted a 6–1 thrashing – including Harry Kane's Panama-hat-trick?

Viewers on big screens were drenched with sunshine then booze as the goals flew in. At Boxpark Croydon and Newcastle's Times Square, hundreds of delirious fans went nuts. Revellers dressed as lions waved replica trophies near London Bridge. And at the Isle of Wight Festival, thousands of music fans celebrated amid clouds of dry ice.

Jubilant fans stepped out of pubs and homes to celebrate in the streets, which began to echo more loudly to the Three Lions song. Traffic on travel and ticket websites surged as confident fans considered joining the 2,500 England fans at the stadium. Even the Auld Enemy caught the England bug – nearly one in four Scottish punters placed money on England to win. Hamish Husband, of the West of Scotland Tartan Army, claimed even if they had, 'nobody would ever admit betting on England. I never watch them. I just hope that they have a bit of fun and lose heavily in the semi-final.'

Gareth Southgate threw a World Cup party for his players at their Repino HQ to celebrate reaching the knockout stages. And the England chief said he wanted a big win over Belgium to top Group G. As his players sank a few pints at the ForRestMix Club after their 6–1 demolition of Panama, Southgate said: 'It's an important moment to get music on and have a couple of beers. I'm enjoying the win, enjoying the fact we've qualified, and then tomorrow we can start the next phase. When I look back, we didn't enjoy qualifying for the World Cup as much as we should have, so we want to get that right.'

Southgate said he wanted to keep up the momentum by beating Belgium, which would have led to a likely quarter-final against Germany or Brazil. He said: 'We want to win every game. I don't know how we would go into a game not wanting to win. For our country, that would be a very difficult mindset to have, and it's dangerous territory if we start trying to predict where we might end up. We all know the quality of the Belgium squad and the individuals they have. But we think we can be competitive in all those games. We're improving, and the lads are gaining belief.'

Midfielder Ruben Loftus-Cheek said the players were only thinking of making it three wins from three. He said: 'We won't fear anyone, and we don't want to take our foot off the gas with the performances we are putting in now.' After missing the Panama game with a thigh problem, Dele Alli took part in full training.

Goal-machine Harry Kane's fiancée was watching his World Cup heroics from a giant wigwam in their garden. Kate Goodland, 25, opted to stay at home with their daughter Ivy so captain Harry could concentrate on leading England to glory. She shared pictures on Instagram of the huge tent in Essex – complete with widescreen TV and decked out with England bunting. There was also a huge poster of the Spurs star with the words the fans sing about the club legend: 'He's one of our own.'

With qualification to the knockout stages assured, players relaxed with yoga before the Belgium match. Ashley Young, Jordan Pickford and Harry Maguire use the ancient Indian discipline as a regular part of their fitness and flexibility regime. Aptly, the lads were pictured performing the 'warrior pose' to help give flexibility in the hips and to strengthen the legs, ankles and feet. The team-mates worked out under a sign that read: 'Success isn't given, it's earned on the track, in the field, in the gym, with blood, sweat and the occasional tear.'

As results unravelled, topping the group became something of a poisoned chalice. Did we really want a quarter-final against five-time World Cup winners Brazil? Debate raged over whether Southgate should maintain the winning momentum or rest vital players. Kane was desperate to maintain his grip on the Golden Boot as the tournament's top scorer – but would Southgate leave out his star man?

ENGLAND CAMP

THURSDAY
28
JUNE

England 0–1 Belgium

Januzaj 51

Gareth Southgate urged England fans to 'look at the bigger picture' after his gamble of fielding a weakened team against Belgium ended in defeat in Kaliningrad. And the Three Lions boss promised that his men would be ready for what he predicted would be a 'thrilling' last-16 showdown with 2014 quarter-finalists Colombia.

With both teams already guaranteed a last-16 spot, the eagerly awaited clash of the Group G big guns turned into a reserve match, with Southgate making eight changes and Belgium boss Roberto Martínez nine. Victory assured Belgium of the top spot and a relatively easier tie against Japan, but it also meant England avoided a potential meeting with Brazil in the quarter-finals.

After seeing his side beaten by a superb Adnan Januzaj goal, Southgate insisted he was right to leave out most of his first-choice stars, including captain Harry Kane. 'This was a game we wanted to win,' he said, 'but the knockout game is the biggest game for a decade, so we needed to make sure our key players were preserved. What we have to do is prepare for a thrilling knockout game. Our objective was to qualify from the group and we've done that. The players gave everything. We kept pressing until the end. I think the supporters understand what the most important thing is. None of us know if this side of the draw is advantageous or not. Everybody is in the frame to play in the next game and it was important these players were given time on the pitch to press their case. Anybody that plays against Colombia will know they are match-ready.'

Being left out denied five-goal skipper Kane the chance to extend his lead at the top of the Golden Boot chart, but Southgate added: 'He was brilliant about it. His priority, like ours, is the team. He recognised what we were trying to do. If we played Harry Kane for 50 minutes tonight and he takes a whack, we would have been foolish. He is a world-class striker and we want him to be ready for Colombia. If we had put Harry on for ten minutes and someone had raked his ankle, that would have been ridiculous. The knockout game is the important one. Of course we have a responsibility to the supporters, and the support in the stadium was absolutely outstanding tonight. The support and the encouragement from home has been brilliant. But when you're a leader and a manager, you have to make decisions that are right for your group to achieve the primary objective. Sometimes those decisions will be criticised. I understand that. But only one person makes that decision with all the full facts and managing a tournament in mind – physically, medically, tactically for the benefit of the group. Sometimes you have to make decisions for the bigger picture.'

Januzaj's winner, after 51 minutes, was a rare moment of quality in a strangely subdued game. Belgium started the stronger, with keeper Jordan Pickford forced into a decent save as early as the sixth minute by a long-range effort from Youri Tielemans. Four minutes later, England survived a big scare. After initially appearing to smother Michy Batshuayi's close-range effort, Pickford allowed the ball to squirm from his grasp and the ball looked set to dribble over the line until Gary Cahill got back to hack it clear.

England responded with a half-chance for Jamie Vardy after 14 minutes. Liverpool teenager Trent Alexander-Arnold broke on the right wing and crossed for Vardy, whose header flashed wide of the post. But Alexander-Arnold had to be alert at the other end after 27 minutes when a Belgian corner caused panic in the England defence. In an almighty scramble in front of keeper Pickford, Fellaini hooked the ball goalwards and Alexander-Arnold was forced to clear off the line. Set-pieces had been England's most successful source of goals in their first two games, and after 34 minutes Ruben Loftus-Cheek got on the end of an Alexander-Arnold corner but could only put his header wide.

'THIS WAS A GAME WE WANTED TO WIN, BUT THE KNOCKOUT GAME IS THE BIGGEST GAME FOR A DECADE, SO WE NEEDED TO MAKE SURE OUR KEY PLAYERS WERE PRESERVED. WHAT WE HAVE TO DO IS PREPARE FOR A THRILLING KNOCKOUT GAME. OUR OBJECTIVE WAS TO QUALIFY FROM THE GROUP AND WE'VE DONE THAT.'

GARETH SOUTHGATE

Early in the second half, England had their best chance yet. Vardy fed the ball to Marcus Rashford, but the Manchester United striker's attempt at a curling shot flew wide. Soon afterwards, former United winger Januzaj showed him how to do it. Cutting in from the right flank, he wrong-footed Danny Rose and whipped a superb shot over the diving Pickford and into the top corner. In the celebrations, Batshuayi gave TV viewers a laugh when he picked up the ball and booted it against the post – only for it to rebound into his face!

England were struggling to wrestle back control of the game, but they had a glorious chance to equalise after 66 minutes when Vardy's perfectly-weighted pass sent Rashford bearing down on the Belgian goal. Rashford was one-on-one with Thibaut Courtois but chose to shoot rather than try to round the keeper, and his attempt to shape the ball into the corner ended with the ball going wide. Courtois got a fingertip on it, but the shot was probably missing anyway.

Although the Three Lions threatened again after 87 minutes when Danny Welbeck flicked an effort wide from close range, it was Belgium who came closest to scoring once more near the end. First, sub Dries Mertens forced Pickford into another save with a dipping shot, then a

Batshuayi run into the box sparked another scramble, with Fellaini and Mertens both unable to apply the finishing touch. To emphasise Belgium's superiority, Thorgan Hazard, brother of their rested star man, Eden, had the last chance, shooting into the side netting after a good move.

England boss Southgate said: 'I think it was a pretty even game. I thought they had the better-controlled possession and the better chances in the first half. But we had a couple of good ones in the second half. So it was a good test for us. Marcus Rashford and Jamie Vardy kept running, but it didn't happen for them tonight. Tonight, we played okay. I don't think anyone played poorly. We didn't have the link between the lines quite as well, but there were good individual moments and a lot we can learn from. We don't like to lose matches, but the primary objectives from the game we have got. Sometimes you have to look at the bigger picture and make decisions that might be criticised. But I think everyone has understood what we are trying to do.'

Southgate admitted the defeat was, in some respects, a welcome reality check. He felt that a victory – despite being against a Belgian second-string team – might have encouraged people to get carried away about England's prospects. However, he insisted he was confident

'AT A WORLD CUP YOU'RE GOING TO COME UP AGAINST THE BEST TEAMS IN THE WORLD. THERE ARE NO EASY GAMES WE CAN SEE AHEAD OF US. COLOMBIA WILL BE VERY TOUGH.'

TRENT ALEXANDER-ARNOLD

England were capable of beating Colombia in the last 16, which would open the way for a quarter-final clash with either Switzerland or Sweden.

He said: 'Colombia have got some outstanding individuals but I believe it's a game we can win. We feel we are a team who are improving. We have levels still to reach and work to do, but that's nothing we didn't already know. That's not a bad thing. If we had won tonight, the reality of where we are might not have been in people's minds. We know where we are. We know how immaculate we have to be to win matches against the best teams and we have that challenge still to come. Whatever happens next week, the selection against Belgium was the right decision as far as I'm concerned. People will say it is only the right decision if we win next week, but we are potentially going into a match with extra-time having risked players here we didn't need to risk. I know this meant the game against Belgium was a little bit flat, but every player in that dressing room knows why we have done what we have done. We are through to the next phase. Okay, we didn't win the game, but there was a myriad of other things involved in this decision. I understand why people question those decisions, but we have to prepare the team in the way we feel is right.'

One bright spot for England was the impressive performance of rookie right-back Alexander-Arnold, who was winning only his second cap. The Liverpool kid was adamant that plotting a supposedly easier route through the knockout stages did not have any bearing on the match. He said: 'I'm very disappointed. We wanted to win the game and we didn't. But at the end of the day we are still in the round of 16, and that is something to look forward to. We had our chances and never took them. They had one big chance and took it. It was a good goal. We can only regret the chances we didn't take. Getting out of the group was the first objective of the team. We are England and we want to win every game possible. You don't want to go into a changing room and see smiles because you've got a potentially easier route. You want to win every game. And at a World Cup you're going to come up against the best teams in the world. There are no easy games we can see ahead of us. Colombia will be very tough. It's not going to be easy at all.'

With penalties now a possibility going into the knockout stages, Southgate confirmed he had been thoroughly preparing the squad for spot-kicks. Southgate, who famously missed the crucial penalty in England's Euro 96 semi-final defeat by Germany, said: 'We've been practising and going through strategies since March. We've done various different studies and had individual practice.'

That practice was about to pay off.

ENGLAND V BELGIUM

ROAROMETER: 40 dB – A library

FOOTBALL TO HOME:
1,143 miles (1,841 km)

V

Against much-fancied Belgium, only group placings were important. The winner could meet Brazil in the quarter-finals – the runner-up Sweden or Switzerland. And the country's mood reflected that. Fans slipped out of work early to get home or pack pubs across the country for what turned out to be a clash of reserve sides.

Two wins out of two had already assured England's place in the second round and the fans' faith was growing. Was it a coincidence that more England flags were fluttering on cars and vans across the country? In Wiltshire, fans placed two huge red ribbons across the historic Westbury White Horse to create a giant St George's Cross flag on the hillside. English Heritage had it removed.

Many probably wished they had not bothered. A flat game was decided by a single goal by Belgium's former Manchester United winger Adnan Januzaj. We lost but went home happy, for a change. Job done. England marched on . . .

THE WORLD CUP ACCORDING TO

The Sun loves the World Cup. Here's a look back at the iconic front and back pages charting England's historic journey in 2018.

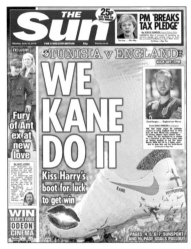

On the day of our opening game against Tunisia, *The Sun* urged readers to kiss the boot of England skipper Harry Kane for luck.

A plague of midges couldn't stop hero Harry bagging two goals. *Sun* readers kissing his boot worked!

The Three Lions got to the knockout stages by scoring six against Panama. We celebrated with our own take on a Hot Chocolate classic.

The Sun urged the Prime Minister to display the St George's Cross flag on the day of the game against Belgium.

England fans celebrated as the German team crashed out in the group stages, deriving pleasure from their misfortune – now, if only there were a word for that?

England's defeat to Belgium meant we didn't win the group – but that was good news as it gave us an easier route to the semis.

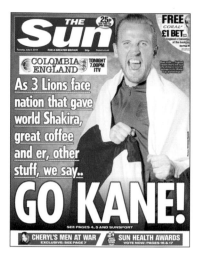

On the day of our match against Colombia, we issued an impassioned, if controversial, rallying cry.

Gareth Southgate warned Kane & Co. not to get carried away as a dream route to the final opened up before them.

Goalie Jordan Pickford was pictured saving the Colombia penalty that helped England win their first World Cup shoot-out.

Our sports writers were finally able to write the headline they had waited a lifetime for!

England beat Sweden and earned a place in the semi-final for the first time since 1990. *The Sun on Sunday* echoed the cry heard across the country.

The nation was focused on the upcoming semi against Croatia when the government decided to implode. We told politicians to pull themselves together!

The splash after the defeat to Croatia reflected the sentiment of England fans across the nation. You did good, lads.

«««

SunSport's take on England's defeat was that the whole 23-man squad were heroes who should have nothing but pride.

»»»

MEANWHILE...
GROUP STAGE EXITS

Champions **GERMANY** were the biggest casualties in a thrilling group stage that set up one of the most exciting World Cups for years. The Germans arrived as one of the favourites but were stunned by an opening 1–0 defeat by **MEXICO**. They kept their hopes alive with a dramatic late goal in a 2–1 victory over **SWEDEN**, only to crash out as already-eliminated **SOUTH KOREA** scored twice in injury time to chalk up a famous 2–0 win.

Incredibly, Germany finished bottom of Group F, and coach Joachim Löw, who led them to the title in 2014, admitted arrogance played a part in their failure. He said: 'We were convinced once the tournament started we would be able to play well, but it didn't happen. Maybe we thought that at the push of a button we could shift gears. We couldn't flip that switch.' The Germans' exit was a boost for England, who knew they might have faced their old enemy in the quarter-finals.

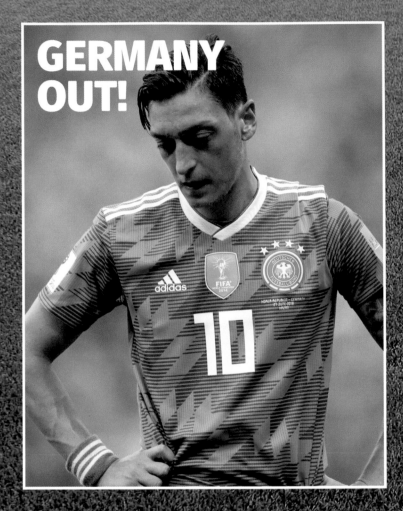

GERMANY OUT!

SPAIN and **PORTUGAL** produced one of the games of the tournament, with Cristiano Ronaldo completing a hat-trick with a brilliant late free-kick in their 3–3 draw. Both teams progressed, despite Portugal drawing 1–1 with Iran and Spain being held 2–2 by Morocco.

While **FRANCE** looked inconsistent in topping Group C ahead of Denmark, **CROATIA** were one of the teams of the first stage, thumping **ARGENTINA** 3–0 on their way to making it three wins from three in Group D. The Argentinians scraped through thanks to a late header from Marcos Rojo in a 2–1 win over **NIGERIA** in their final game – and the watching Diego Maradona celebrated by swearing at fans and giving them the finger.

Hosts **RUSSIA**, widely written off as no-hopers, surprised many people by qualifying behind the impressive **URUGUAY** from Group A, while the unlucky Mo Salah's hopes of lighting up the tournament with **EGYPT** were wrecked by the shoulder injury he suffered during Liverpool's Champions League Final defeat.

Even **BRAZIL** didn't have it all their own way, drawing 1–1 with **SWITZERLAND** in their opener and only assuring themselves of qualification as Group E winners by seeing off **SERBIA** 2–0 in their final match. Switzerland joined them in the last 16, thanks largely to a 2–1 win over Serbia in their second game, which sparked one of the big controversies of the tournament. Swiss duo Granit

Xhaka and Xherdan Shaqiri, both of whom have Albanian heritage, were fined after making the nationalist double-headed eagle symbol with their hands after scoring.

The tightest group of all was Group H, where **COLOMBIA** recovered from losing their opening game to **JAPAN** to finish top. In a dramatic and controversial finale to the group, Colombia's 1–0 win over

SENEGAL meant Japan scraped through in second ahead of the Africans because they had had fewer yellow cards. Trailing 1–0 to already-eliminated **POLAND**, Japan gambled by playing keep-ball for the last 15 minutes of their game in the knowledge they would go through if Senegal didn't equalise against Colombia.

SENEGAL OUT!

As the England squad jetted back to their training camp in Repino, the mood was downcast. The team had suffered their first defeat in the World Cup, losing 1–0 to Belgium and finishing the group stage as runners-up. It was the first setback on the road to glory after beating Tunisia and Panama in their opening games.

Was this a reality check for the Three Lions? Fans didn't seem to think so. The loss arguably put England on an easier path to the semi-finals. By finishing second in Group G behind Belgium, we would face Colombia – avoiding previous World Cup winners Brazil, France and Argentina on the other side of the draw.

Fans had other reasons to celebrate. Gareth Southgate had deliberately played a second-string side, resting key players like Harry Kane so they would be fitter for the round of 16. Southgate said: 'The knockout game is our biggest for a decade, so we had to make sure our key players were preserved.' But there were worries over lost momentum. Should they have played a stronger team and topped the group?

The squad didn't dwell on decisions made for the Belgium game. Photos emerged of smiling Three Lions players as they took part in a recovery session. Eric Dier and Dele Alli laughed as they knelt in an ice bath, and Jesse Lingard and Ashley Young were seen stretching in the training camp's pool. Several players, including Lingard and Marcus Rashford, took a rollercoaster ride at a local theme park on their day off.

Dele Alli looked in good shape training on an exercise bike after picking up a thigh injury, which meant he had to sit out two of the three group games. Fabian Delph missed training as he jetted home to be by wife Natalie's side for the birth of his third daughter. The team were super-fit, ready to play 30 minutes of extra time against Colombia if it came down to it.

But the question hanging in the air as the first knockout match loomed was whether England could break their penalty shoot-out jinx. The Three Lions had lost six out of seven shoot-outs at major tournaments. England famously didn't win on penalties – the players knew it and the fans knew it.

Nobody was more experienced in the pain of missing from the spot than Southgate, who had spent 22 years brooding over that fateful miss against Germany in Euro 96, which knocked England out of the tournament. He said: 'It's not about luck, it's about performing a skill under pressure. I have had a couple of decades thinking it through.'

The gaffer had psychologically profiled his players to make sure they were up for it. Members of the squad had sat psychometric tests to measure mental strength and took daily wellness questionnaires, supervised by a psychologist.

Could the man who famously mocked his own miss in a Pizza Hut advert be the person who could break England's penalty curse?

ENGLAND CAMP

TUESDAY

03

JULY

Colombia 1–1 England

Y. Mina 90+3   Kane 57 (pen.)

England win 4–3 on penalties

Eric Dier hailed 'fantastic' keeper Jordan Pickford after the pair ended England's penalty-shoot-out curse to seal a heart-stopping win over Colombia. Pickford's stunning save and Dier's decisive spot-kick ended the Three Lions' run of five successive shoot-out defeats and set up a quarter-final date with Sweden.

In a fiery and thrilling last-16 battle in Moscow, England appeared to have blown it when a last-gasp goal from Yerry Mina cancelled out captain Harry Kane's penalty and forced the tie into extra time. But England battled back from that devastating setback to take it all the way to penalties, then held their nerve to pull off a first shoot-out victory since beating Spain at Euro 96.

Another spot-kick disaster seemed to be on the cards when Jordan Henderson saw his penalty saved by David Ospina, but England got a reprieve when Mateus Uribe smashed his effort against the bar, and, after Kieran Trippier levelled the scores at 3–3, Pickford brilliantly kept out Carlos Bacca's penalty. That left Dier with the chance to win it, and he buried his shot low into the corner despite Ospina getting a glove on it.

Sub Dier said: 'Jordan is a fantastic goalkeeper with a fantastic attitude, and he deserves everything. He was fantastic in the penalty shoot-out. He's big in goal, he's been brilliant in training and he has taken it into the game.' The Tottenham midfielder was told by Southgate he had to take the fifth penalty because Jamie Vardy had picked up a groin injury after coming on. Dier said: 'I don't really know what I was thinking about at the time, to be honest. While you're waiting to take it, it's nerve-racking. But once I walked up, when I was going to take it I was quite calm. I was very nervous while standing waiting, but once I walked up there I was all right.' Dier had missed a headed chance in extra time and admitted: 'I felt like I had to score after that header I missed at the end. I'm thankful I scored it. I've never really been in that situation before.'

Everton keeper Pickford had been criticised after a shaky performance against Belgium, with their No. 1, Thibaut Courtois, claiming that, at 6ft 1in, Pickford wasn't tall enough to be a top-class keeper.

Pickford said: 'I don't care if I'm not the biggest keeper, but I've got the power and agility to help me get around the goal and I'm very good at it. It's about making the save and being in the moment. I might be young, but I've got good mental strength and experience and I used that today. It's a great night. If it had to go to penalties we knew we were capable of winning. Ideally, we don't want to be going to a penalty shoot-out but we are delighted for the fans and the whole country.'

Liverpool star Henderson admitted he was relieved to be bailed out by Pickford. He said: 'I thanked him. I can't thank him enough. I'm forever in his debt. We're a really close group. I think you can see that. But it's difficult when you miss. Nothing can be said that's going to make it all right. Jordan got a bit of criticism last week, undeservedly so. I'm happy for him to achieve that tonight.'

Boss Gareth Southgate said: 'Fantastic! Today was a special night for every Englishman. We're trying to write our own history and I have talked to the players about that. They write their own stories. We don't have to be bowed by the pressure of the past. This was special, but I want us to go on. I don't want to go home yet. We deserved it, as well. We played so well in the 90 minutes. We showed huge resilience to come back from huge disappointment and kept calm. Shoot-outs are tough. We had talked long and hard about owning the process of a shoot-out. They kept calm. We looked at technique, how we need to be as a team, the goalkeeper's role. It's a special moment. But now I'm thinking about Sweden. They're another team we have a poor record against. We have underestimated them for years.'

After fielding a weakened team against Belgium, Southgate picked the XI who started against Tunisia, with fit-again Dele Alli reclaiming his place from Ruben Loftus-Cheek, and the lethargy of the Belgian defeat was quickly forgotten as the Three Lions dominated from the start. Despite England being on top, the closest they came in the first half was when Kane headed over from a Trippier cross after 16 minutes. Colombia, who suffered a hammer blow before the game when 2014 Golden Boot winner James Rodríguez was ruled out with a calf injury, seemed intent on using dirty tricks to unsettle Southgate's team, and five minutes before half-time they were lucky not to be reduced to ten men when Wílmar Barrios headbutted Henderson as England prepared to take a free-kick. Incredibly, American referee Mike Geiger showed him only a yellow card after appearing to take advice through his headset from the VAR team.

England continued to look the better team at the start of the second half and, after 54 minutes, ref Geiger pointed to the spot when Carlos Sánchez wrestled Kane to the ground as Ashley Young floated a free-kick into the box. Extraordinary scenes followed, with the Colombians delaying the penalty for several minutes with their furious protests. Johan Mojica even scuffed up the penalty spot with his boot during the melée and England star Henderson was booked as tempers boiled over. But the calmest man in the Spartak Stadium was Kane, and he smashed his penalty down the middle as Ospina dived to his right, making it six

'I WAS VERY NERVOUS WHILE STANDING WAITING, BUT ONCE I WALKED UP THERE I WAS ALL RIGHT. I FELT LIKE I HAD TO SCORE AFTER THAT HEADER I MISSED AT THE END.'

ERIC DIER

goals for the tournament – as many as Gary Lineker's Golden Boot-winning haul in 1986.

As the half wore on, England began to fade and they survived a huge scare after 81 minutes when Kyle Walker blundered, losing the ball on the halfway line. But Colombia's counter-attack ended with Cuadrado blazing his shot over. With three minutes of injury time played, there was relief as Mateus Uribe unleashed a fantastic long-range dipper and Pickford acrobatically turned it around the post. The reprieve was short-lived, though, as Mina leapt above Maguire from the resulting corner to score with a downward header that bounced up and in off the bar, despite Trippier's desperate attempt to head it off the line.

It was a devastating setback and, in the first half of extra time, it showed as Colombia enjoyed their best spell of the game. Shortly before the end of the first period, Radamel Falcao came close to making it 2–1, heading wide under pressure from Maguire. England weathered the storm and, in the second period, sub Danny Rose fired a shot wide as the Three Lions went back on the offensive. With five minutes left, Dier headed over a golden chance from a corner. That proved to be the final opportunity and it was down to penalties.

Falcao and Cuadrado scored the first two for Colombia, with Kane and Rashford responding. But after Luis Muriel had rolled his spot-kick past Pickford, it was advantage Colombia when Henderson saw his sidefooted effort brilliantly saved by Ospina. However, just as England fans feared the worst, Uribe hit the crossbar and Trippier fired his shot into the top corner to level it up. Suddenly the shoot-out swung decisively in England's favour. Bacca shot down the middle and, despite diving to his right, Pickford somehow reached up in mid-flight and palmed the ball out. The stage was set for Dier to break the jinx and he made no mistake, shooting low into the corner to spark wild celebrations among the England players.

Captain Kane praised his team for fighting back after the shock of conceding a late equaliser. He said: 'We controlled the game and it hits you hard when something like that happens. But it shows what we're made of. We had to go again in extra time and then the penalty shoot-out. It's been terrible for us over the years – of course we know that – and to step up when it mattered and do what we did, I'm so proud of everyone involved.'

Fellow Tottenham star Trippier, whose penalty got England back in the shoot-out, said: 'We've practised after loads of training sessions when we've been fatiguing. I had full faith in all the boys. With my penalty, I just stick to one spot and put it there. I believe in my own

'I HAD FULL FAITH IN ALL THE BOYS. WITH MY PENALTY, I JUST STICK TO ONE SPOT AND PUT IT THERE. I BELIEVE IN MY OWN ABILITY AND I BELIEVED THAT I COULD SCORE.'

KIERAN TRIPPIER

ability and I believed that I could score. Hendo missed but we are all behind him and we couldn't be happier for Picks and Eric.' Pickford said he had done 'a lot of research' on the Colombian penalty-takers, and his understudy Jack Butland revealed that the England keeper even had a water bottle with tips on each taker written on it.

The game was marred by Colombia's antics, and Leicester defender Maguire claimed: 'They did everything they could to frustrate us – falling on the floor, rolling about and continuous fouling. It was a tough game to get any rhythm. We controlled the game for the 90 minutes, then the big sucker punch at the end. Maybe we should deal with the corner better. They threw bodies in the box and it was a bit difficult to take. We could have quite easily gone under at that point, but the boys showed great courage and character to come back.'

Boss Southgate praised his team for keeping their discipline in the face of provocation and a hostile atmosphere. He said: 'We didn't rise to it in general, which was brilliant. A couple of times we lost our cool. It looked like our fans were outnumbered five to one. It was an away game. To deal with it all was exceptional. There were many, many fouls in the game and I don't think we committed anywhere near the number they did. We kept our composure in a really difficult environment.'

'TODAY WAS A SPECIAL NIGHT FOR EVERY ENGLISHMAN.

WE'RE TRYING TO WRITE OUR OWN HISTORY.'

ENGLAND V COLOMBIA

ROAROMETER: 135 dB – Air-raid siren

FOOTBALL TO HOME:
1,828 miles (2,942 km)

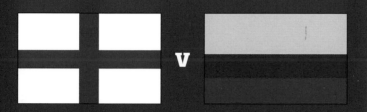 V

Meltdown as 23.8 million ecstatic fans watching on TV celebrate England's first penalty shoot-out win at a World Cup. Harry Kane's penalty looked enough until Colombia's late equaliser brought extra time and dreaded pens. But Jordan Pickford's save and Eric Dier's kick reduced ITV pundit Ian Wright to tears.

🐦 @GaryLineker
I'm crying. Yes yes yes.

🐦 @KensingtonRoyal
I couldn't be prouder of @england – a victory in a penalty shoot-out! You have well and truly earned your place in the final eight of the #worldcup and you should know the whole country is right behind you for Saturday! Come on England! W

🐦 @RollingStones

Hours earlier, roads had been deserted. By 10.15pm in London, fans singing 'Football's Coming Home' stopped traffic on London's Shoreditch High Street. It was the same in Leeds, Newcastle and even Brighton's sea front. On the Kirby estate in Bermondsey, England and Colombia fans watched together. Around 36 million pints were sunk in pubs across the country, and social media showed fans celebrating in bars, streets and on bus roofs.

Over-excited James Read apologised on Twitter for 'celebrating winning by accidentally elbowing my 71-year-old mother in the face. Sorry Mum!' Kensington Palace tweeted the Duke of Cambridge's congratulations. Wimbledon bosses refused to show the match on the big screen at Murray Mound. 'We're a tennis event and that's what people come to see,' sniffed a spokesman.

Love Island fans moaned when ITV held the show back to 10pm. One quipped: 'It's crazy. Megan could have ruined three relationships in that time.'

THE PENALTY SHOOT-OUT

1

FALCAO
SCORED!

2

JUAN
CUADRADO
SCORED!

3

MURIEL
SCORED!

1

KANE
SCORED!

2

RASHFORD
SCORED!

3

HENDERSON
MISSED!

> **'WE HAD TALKED LONG AND HARD ABOUT OWNING THE PROCESS OF A SHOOT-OUT.'**
>
> GARETH SOUTHGATE

4 URIBE
MISSED!

5 BACCA
MISSED!

4 TRIPPIER
SCORED!

5 DIER
SCORED!

ENGLAND AND PENALTIES – FROM HELL TO HEAVEN

WE didn't win the trophy – but we did win a World Cup penalty shoot-out and end 22 years of hurt. On a historic night in Moscow, Jordan Pickford's brilliant one-handed save from Colombia's Carlos Bacca set up Eric Dier to score and send England into the quarter-finals. We had won just one out of the seven previous tournament shoot-outs – but with one kick our record went from dire to Dier. And the curse was lifted.

The transformation was redemption for manager Gareth Southgate, whose semi-final shoot-out miss against Germany sent England out of Euro 96. Southgate – who admitted he just wanted his own kick over and done with – took a scientific approach. He made players walk from the halfway line before their kick during training and used sports psychologists to help the players 'own the process'. And they were even smart enough to smuggle notes to Pickford about the Colombia kickers on a water bottle before the shoot-out began.

So next time we face penalties the players – and the nation – can think of a success story instead of all those failures. And maybe we can go the whole 12 yards and win the World Cup.

England 3 West Germany 4
World Cup semi-final
4 July 1990, Stadio delle Alpi, Turin

After a pulsating 120 minutes, inspired England – in their biggest match since 1966 – had drawn 1–1 with Germany. Gary Lineker, Peter Beardsley and David Platt scored. Stuart Pearce's effort was saved by Bodo Illgner. Chris Waddle blazed a shot high over the bar. The nightmare had begun.

England 4 Spain 2
Euro 96 quarter-final
22 June 1996, Wembley

England's only win for another 22 years. Terry Venables' side had dazzled during the group stages. But resilient Spain held them to a 0–0 draw after extra time. Fernando Hierro missed, and Alan Shearer, David Platt, Stuart Pearce and Paul Gascoigne all scored before keeper David Seaman saved Miguel Nadal's kick to set up a semi-final against Germany. So we're bound to go out. . .

England 5 Germany 6
Euro 96 semi-final
26 June 1996, Wembley

After 10 successful spot-kicks – Alan Shearer, David Platt, Stuart Pearce, Paul Gascoigne and Teddy Sheringham for England – future England boss Gareth Southgate shoots weakly at Andreas Köpke. Southgate recalled: 'All I wanted was to get the ball, put it on the spot, and get it over and done with.' The curse is working.

England 3 Belgium 4
King Hassan II International Cup
29 May 1998, at Stade Mohammed
V, Casablanca

England warmed up in Morocco for the 1998 World Cup and drew 0–0 with Belgium. Rob Lee's opener was saved but Michael Owen, David Beckham and Paul Merson scored. Les Ferdinand's miss handed the trophy to the Belgians.

England 3 Argentina 4
World Cup Round of 16
30 June 1998, Stade Geoffroy-Guichard,
Saint-Étienne

Brave England are down to ten men after David Beckham's red card for a silly kick on Diego Simeone. Sol Campbell's 81st-minute headed goal is disallowed because of an elbow on the keeper by Alan Shearer. So after extra time, it's penalties. Alan Shearer scores but Paul Ince's effort is saved by Carlos Roa. Paul Merson and Michael Owen score. Roa saves again from David Batty. We're coming home.

England 5 Portugal 6
European Championships quarter-final
24 June 2004, Estádio da Luz, Lisbon

Wayne Rooney has powered England through the group matches, but in the 27th minute he breaks a metatarsal and is subbed. Michael Owen's early strike is cancelled out by Hélder Postiga in the 83rd minute. After extra time it's 2–2. The agony begins as David Beckham shoots over the bar. Michael Owen, Frank Lampard, John Terry, Owen Hargreaves and Ashley Cole score before Portuguese keeper Ricardo changes everything – he stops Darius Vassell's kick, then scores the winner.

England 1 Portugal 3
World Cup quarter-final
1 July 2006, Arena
AufSchalke, Gelsenkirchen

Sven-Göran Eriksson's side crash out after a 0–0 clash with Portugal. Wayne Rooney's red card leaves them down to 10 men for half an hour of normal time and then extra time. Ricardo is again the hero, saving Frank Lampard's opener. He can't stop Owen Hargreaves but foils Steven Gerrard and Jamie Carragher. Cristiano Ronaldo fires the winner. This was our worst shoot-out yet.

England 2 Italy 4
European Championships quarter-final
24 June 2012, Olimpiyskiy National Sports Complex, Kiev

After a gruelling 0–0 draw, Steven Gerrard and Wayne Rooney score, Ashley Young hits the bar and Buffon saves Ashley Cole's strike. There's no end in sight to the hoodoo.

England 4 Colombia 3
World Cup round of 16
3 July 2018, Spartak Stadium, Moscow

Colombia score in added time to cancel out Harry Kane's 57th-minute penalty. England battle on through extra time and face the ordeal . . . but this time with a different ending. Cool Kane nets again, followed by Marcus Rashford. When Jordan Henderson's kick is saved, England look doomed. But Colombia's Mateus Uribe hits the bar, Kieran Trippier scores and keeper Jordan Pickford stops Carlos Bacca's fierce drive with his left hand. Eric Dier scores and England are through. Bring on a shoot-out in the final! Or maybe not . . .

PUB QUIZ PENALTY FACTS

 England have taken 45 shoot-out penalties. We've scored 30 and missed 15. That's a 66.7 per cent success rate.

 We've only missed the target three times – hitting the bar once (Ashley Young v Italy in 2012) and shooting over twice (Chris Waddle v West Germany in 1990 and David Beckham v Portugal in 2004).

 David Platt, Alan Shearer and Michael Owen are our best takers, with three successes each.

 England players who have missed
Gareth Southgate, Stuart Pearce, David Beckham, Chris Waddle, Jamie Carragher, David Batty, Paul Ince, Les Ferdinand, Darius Vassell, Jordan Henderson, Rob Lee, Steven Gerrard, Ashley Cole, Frank Lampard and Ashley Young.

 Scorers
3: David Platt, Michael Owen, Alan Shearer.
2: Owen Hargreaves, Paul Gascoigne, Stuart Pearce, Paul Merson.
1: Gary Lineker, Wayne Rooney, Teddy Sheringham, Peter Beardsley, John Terry, Harry Kane, Marcus Rashford, Kieran Trippier, Eric Dier, Frank Lampard, David Beckham, Ashley Cole, Steven Gerrard.

 We've had 12 penalties saved by opposition keepers – England keepers have saved only four.

Except for one shoot-out – against Spain in 1996 – at least one of our shots is always saved.

Our worst opponents are Portugal, who beat us in 2004 and 2006, and Germany, who beat us in 1990 and 1996.

Portugal keeper Ricardo saved four England penalties – from Darius Vassell in 2004 and Frank Lampard, Steven Gerrard and Jamie Carragher in 2006. He scored the goal that won the 2004 shoot-out.

The first penalty shoot-out was held in the European Championships in 1976 – we didn't qualify.

Penalty missers Gareth Southgate, Chris Waddle and Stuart Pearce cashed in on their misfortune by making TV commercials for Pizza Hut in 1996!

MEANWHILE...
ROUND OF 16 EXITS

Superstars Lionel Messi and Cristiano Ronaldo waved goodbye to the World Cup for possibly the last time as the big names continued to fall. While England fans were really starting to believe, Messi's **ARGENTINA** and Ronaldo's **PORTUGAL** joined **SPAIN** in falling at the last-16 stage. The second round kicked off in sensational style with the World Cup's Super Saturday as **FRANCE** edged out Argentina 4-3 in a classic and **URUGUAY** saw off European champions Portugal 2-1.

SPAIN OUT!

ARGENTINA OUT!

Argentina's campaign was overshadowed by a player revolt against coach Jorge Sampaoli during the group stage, and when they needed captain Messi most of all he came up short. Instead, the star turn was French teenager Kylian Mbappé, the 19-year-old becoming the first teenager to score twice in a World Cup finals match since Pelé in the 1958 final.

France coach Didier Deschamps, whose team fought back from 2-1 down, said: 'Our team is younger, but we answered the call. We have a lot of character and it wasn't easy. We kept fighting. We did everything to go further.' Messi walked down the tunnel with head bowed at the end, realising that, at 31, this was likely to be his last shot at winning the World Cup.

The same applied to 33-year-old Ronaldo, whose Portugal were downed by two-goal Uruguay hero Edinson Cavani. Ronaldo said: 'I'm leaving here content because things went pretty well in general. We're going out with our heads held high. It's not the time to talk about the future. As captain I'm proud of the players.'

Spain's shock exit on penalties to hosts **RUSSIA** ended a campaign that had begun in a state of turmoil, with coach Julen Lopetegui being sacked before their opening game when it emerged he had agreed to join Real Madrid after the World Cup. Fernando Hierro, who took over on the eve of the tournament, quit after his team's defeat. He insisted the Lopetegui drama was not to blame. He said: 'We all tried our best. I don't think you can talk about the team breaking down or collapsing. There is a fine line between winning and losing.'

Spain had been the only other previous World Cup winners left in **ENGLAND**'s half of the draw, and **SWEDEN**'s 1-0 win over **SWITZERLAND** meant they would face the Three Lions in the quarter-final. The winners knew they would tackle either **CROATIA** – who came through a penalty shootout against **DENMARK** – or Russia in the last four.

On the other side of the draw, goals from Neymar and Roberto Firmino gave **BRAZIL** a 2-0 win over **MEXICO**. That set up a quarter-final with **BELGIUM**, whose Golden Generation survived a huge scare against **JAPAN**. The Japanese led 2-0 with just 21 minutes left, but the Belgians fought back to win 3-2 with an injury-time winner from Nacer Chadli. Belgium coach Roberto Martínez said: 'There is something special in this squad – no doubt about it. The signs are positive. We can't wait to face Brazil. We are as ready as we can be. Over the last two years we have been working towards this moment.'

JAPAN OUT!

IN THE

The curse had been broken. Gareth Southgate and his five penalty-takers had made history. The Three Lions had roared into the quarter-finals, finally putting an end to so many years of bad luck. It was almost worth sacrificing a 1–0 lead in the 93rd minute to see this.

Midfielder Fabian Delph had missed the Colombia game, having been given leave to fly home for the birth of his daughter straight after the group defeat against Belgium. When he arrived back at Repino on Wednesday as the proud dad of three, he was given a new England shirt by the FA – a tiny one for his new little girl, emblazoned with DELPH 17 on the back. Fabian posted on Instagram: 'I've just experienced the most amazing 24 hours. Can't put into words the happiness and gratitude I'm feeling.'

With all the squad back at camp, thoughts turned to Saturday's upcoming knockout game against Sweden. The path to a World Cup Final seemed clear – England had a realistic shot at lifting the trophy for the first time in a generation. Defender Harry Maguire said: 'Is this our best chance to win a tournament? Definitely. We are hungry, we are fearless and the boys have shown great character.' But England's record against Sweden suggested that this wouldn't be a walkover. In 24 meetings we had only won eight times, with nine draws.

The Swedish team tore into their rivals. Captain Andreas Granqvist sneered at claims that England were favourites. Former Swedish international Håkan Mild also slammed the Three Lions. He said: 'They think they are so good but they are not. It's spoilt young people who make a ton of money . . . They think they are going to win and will get an unpleasant surprise on Saturday.' The cries were echoed by a former England manager, Swede Sven-Göran Eriksson, who managed England at two World Cups. He said: 'It'll be the most difficult game they'll have played so far. Sweden won't be impressed by Harry Kane or whoever is in the England team.'

Calm Southgate refused to be dragged into a war of words. He said: 'It will be a tough game, because Sweden are often underestimated, and I have real respect for them. They are always more than the sum of their parts. Our historic record against them is another one we have to put right. I think we have always viewed them at our level and I don't think that's right, because their tournament record is better than ours.'

Questions were also being raised about the fitness of the England side, who had gone the distance with Colombia less than a week earlier. Ashley Young had suffered a thigh strain and taken a knock to the ankle. Harry Kane, John Stones and Kyle Walker had cramped up. Jamie Vardy was absent from training with a groin strain. And doubts hung over Dele Alli, who recovered from a thigh injury to face Colombia but had to go off with nine minutes left.

Yet the team were buoyed by the huge surge of support at home. Excitement was at fever-pitch, pubs were expecting record turnouts and the weather forecast was glorious. Wedding plans were being hastily rearranged to enable guests to watch the game. The National Grid warned of an electricity spike at half-time as supporters opened fridge doors to grab a beer.

England had not progressed to a World Cup semi-final since 1990, so beating Sweden would see the young lions make more history in Russia.

QUARTER-FINALS

SATURDAY

07

JULY

Sweden 0–2 England

Maguire 30
Alli 59

Gareth Southgate said his young team were 'maturing before our eyes' after England reached the World Cup semi-finals for only the third time in their history. After the drama of the last-16 penalty shootout win over Colombia, this was a relative stroll, as goals from Harry Maguire and Dele Alli booked a Moscow meeting with Croatia. Although the Three Lions needed three top-class saves from keeper Jordan Pickford, they thoroughly deserved their victory, with Sweden coach Janne Andersson tipping them to go all the way.

Southgate, who again enjoyed what was becoming his trademark double-fist-pump celebration in front of the England fans after the game, said: 'I hope everyone at home enjoys tonight, because it's not often this happens. We knew it was going to be such a different game after having extra time and penalties against Colombia, with all the emotion and energy. We had to withstand a lot of physical pressure but the resilience of the team was crucial.'

Harry Maguire broke the deadlock with a header from a corner in the first half, before Dele Alli headed in a Jesse Lingard cross to make the final half-hour a near formality. Sweden tried to fight back, but Jordan Pickford made sure England registered their first clean sheet of the tournament.

Southgate explained: 'We knew we would have the majority of the ball and it was a case of breaking them down, because Sweden are a really well-organised team. The question was whether we *could* break them down. We had identified a few areas where we might do that, and we got the goals from them. Sweden make things tough and over the years we have underestimated them. Today, our spirit was as good as theirs but our quality was a little bit better. We have got to this point because the collective has been strong. To have gone to the depths emotionally and physically in midweek, and controlled this game and withstood the physical test, was a sign of the resilience of a young team who are maturing in front of our eyes.

'I spoke to the lads today,' he continued, 'and none of us fancied going home. Now we have to be here another week. It's up to us now which games we play in. In years to come, they will be stronger. But this was a huge opportunity for us and not something we wanted to miss out on.'

The game got off to a cagey start, and the first real sign of danger for Sweden came after 19 minutes – a Raheem Sterling run caused panic and he laid the ball off to Harry Kane, but the captain dragged his shot wide. Gradually, England began to impose their passing game, and it was no surprise that the breakthrough came from a corner, something with which the Three Lions had been so successful in their run to the last eight. Maguire had threatened to score on several occasions in earlier games, and this time there was no denying him as he rose to meet Ashley Young's delivery and powered a header past Robin Olsen.

England appeared increasingly comfortable and Raheem Sterling looked the man most likely to add to their advantage. A superb chipped pass from Kieran Trippier picked him out on the edge of the box, but Manchester United defender Victor Lindelöf did well to nick the ball off his toe as he prepared to shoot. Sterling – without an England goal since October 2015 – was sent clear again by a Lingard pass but shot straight at the keeper. This time the offside flag went up to spare his blushes. Just before the break, he had his best chance of all. Jordan Henderson played him in with a clipped pass over the top and the Manchester City forward had only keeper Olsen to beat. Sterling tried to skip past him, but the keeper got a hand on the ball and, as it broke loose, Sterling's shot from a difficult angle was deflected wide.

If England thought they were in for an easy ride in the second half, they got a wake-up call inside two minutes of the restart when Marcus Berg climbed above Ashley Young at the far post and his powerful downward header forced Pickford into a tremendous Gordon Banks-like save, diving low to his left to scoop the ball away at the foot of his near post.

As in the first half, England steadily warmed to their task and it was after 59 minutes, during their best spell of the game, that they doubled their advantage. When a Lingard shot was blocked, the ball fell to Trippier on the right. He laid it back to Lingard just outside the area, and he clipped a delightful first-time cross to the far post where Alli was onside and unmarked, and made no mistake with a firm header.

As the England fans celebrated behind the goal and Southgate hugged assistant Steve Holland, the PA system at the Samara Arena blasted out Baddiel and Skinner's 'Three Lions' anthem. Sweden weren't going to go down without a fight, however, and after 62 minutes Pickford had to get down low to get a strong hand behind Viktor Claesson's strike from ten yards before a brilliant block by Henderson repelled the follow-up.

Maguire had a chance to put the game to bed after 66 minutes. Henderson headed a corner back across goal, but the Leicester defender ballooned his shot over the bar. Six minutes later, Pickford had to make another top save, tipping the ball over when Berg fired in a shot on the turn. That was the Swedes' last big chance, and England comfortably saw out the final stages to book their place in the last four.

'TO HAVE GONE TO THE DEPTHS EMOTIONALLY AND PHYSICALLY IN MIDWEEK, AND CONTROLLED THIS GAME AND WITHSTOOD THE PHYSICAL TEST, WAS A SIGN OF THE RESILIENCE OF A YOUNG TEAM WHO ARE MATURING IN FRONT OF OUR EYES.'

GARETH SOUTHGATE

Hero keeper Pickford said: 'It's a great result. We knew it was going to be difficult against Sweden. We knew what they were going to bring to the party and we knew we had to bring our A-game. After I made the first save from Berg it set me up for the rest of the game.' Paying tribute to the atmosphere created by several thousand England fans inside the stadium, the Everton keeper added: 'It was quality. England fans are different class. We really enjoy playing and when the fans are like that it makes us very relaxed. I think the last time England were in a semi-final was 1990 – and I wasn't born then. We can go and create our own history.'

Alli, who became England's second-youngest goalscorer at a World Cup behind Michael Owen, said: 'It's always nice to score, especially on an occasion like this, but personally I didn't think it was one of my better games. But to get a goal is unbelievable and it's an amazing feeling to get to the semi-finals. It's a great achievement for the team. We owed it to the fans back home, because we've seen how they are supporting us.'

Captain Kane said: 'I thought we were fantastic. Sweden made it tough – long balls from the back, lots of crosses. We're buzzing with the result! We know there's still a big game ahead – we just have to do it again. We're enjoying it. We've got to keep doing what we're doing and make the country proud.'

Sweden coach Andersson reflected: 'What went wrong? I'm not sure anything went wrong as such. England were the best team today. It's not always that something goes wrong. Sometimes your opponent is better. We were faced with a really good opponent and we didn't reach peak performance. The margins are quite small. There were very few openings generally from the English. We had things under control until they had that corner. I have the greatest respect for England. I definitely believe they're good enough to win it. They're forceful, well organised. They're a good footballing side. I think they would be perfectly able to go all the way.'

England boss Southgate added: 'It's an incredible privilege to be the England manager, but when you sit and think about the people who have got to this point before, people I hugely respect and admire, it's difficult to put into perspective really. It would be fairly easily my best day in coaching. To be in charge of people who give as much energy – and give me as much as they have over this period of time – is very special. It hasn't always been like this when representing England. You only have to go back 18 months, and I said to them that having some kind of success with England would be so much bigger than any success they would enjoy with their clubs. That is maybe starting to register now.'

Roy Hodgson was vilified after England crashed out to Iceland at Euro 2016, but Southgate insisted he deserved credit for gambling on taking some emerging players to that tournament. He said: 'They didn't have big-match experience two years ago and, under pressure, they suffered. Roy took a lot of criticism, but he was brave enough to put them in and deserves credit for that. Without that experience, we wouldn't be here. The experiences two years ago put a lot of those lads in better stead. They are two years further on and have benefited from that as well.

'There is a humility about them, a recognition of where they were 18 months ago and the work that was needed to get them where they are now. These guys are all England fans. Some have been at tournaments in the past as supporters. If not, their families have. They have all worn the shirt as kids and are now proud to wear the shirt as players. As a group, they are tighter. A lot have come through the junior teams together and they have been able to park their club rivalries at the door.'

'IT'S A GREAT ACHIEVEMENT FOR THE TEAM. WE OWED IT TO THE FANS BACK HOME, BECAUSE WE'VE SEEN HOW THEY ARE SUPPORTING US.'

DELE ALLI

ENGLAND V SWEDEN

ROAROMETER: 150 dB – Fighter-jet launch

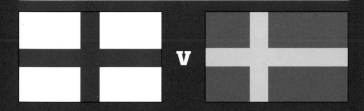

FOOTBALL TO HOME:
2,487 miles (4,004 km)

V

The sun shone. The beer was cold. But we were only supposed to reach the quarter-finals. So victory sent confidence soaring as high as the spray from thousands of plastic pint glasses hurled in the air when Harry Maguire and Dele Alli scored. As 5,000 England fans roared the team on in Russia, back home 32 million watched in homes, pubs and clubs on TV, big screens, mobiles and laptops.

Fans queued for hours to get the best spots in front of big screens – then went wild in Newcastle, Croydon, Brighton, Bristol, Birmingham, Nottingham and London's Trafalgar Square. In Nantwich, Cheshire, fans wore waistcoats in homage to Gareth Southgate. Some dressed down instead – one topless woman clung to a lamppost near London Bridge.

Some went too far, storming Ikea at Stratford, East London. And an ambulance was damaged at Borough Market, London. In Clapham, a bus shelter collapsed under one fan's weight. The RAC declared this the quietest Saturday afternoon of the year as families held World Cup barbecues in 86°F (30°C) heat. But the London Ambulance Service appealed for fans to calm down as 999 calls rocketed.

OUR FANS IN RUSSIA WITH LOVE

They had been warned of marauding ultras and a hostile reception from locals following the Salisbury poisoning scandal. Instead, the 2,000 intrepid Three Lions fans who journeyed to remote Volgograd for the opening game were welcomed with hugs and high fives by an army of Russians in England strips.

Inside the impressive Volgograd Arena, English and Russian fans stood shoulder to shoulder and belted out favourites 'Don't Take Me Home' and the theme tune from *The Great Escape*. It was a plague of midges drifting off the nearby Volga River that proved most troubling to fans and players alike. Brickie Terry Matson, 57, from Sittingbourne, Kent, insisted: 'The only aggro we've had is from the midges.' The Arsenal fan, together with son Jordan, 28, was flying back home the following day to do three days' work on a Kent building site before returning to Russia for the Panama game. A veteran of eight World Cups following England, Terry said: 'We've had a great welcome from the Russians and can't wait to get back out here. It's a pity there weren't more England

fans here tonight, but the support from the Russians made up for it.'

Wearing a plastic British police helmet, an England strip and with the Manchester United crest tattooed on his leg, Moscow restaurant boss Max Mavlytov, 34, revealed: 'I love England and the English. I've watched England play in Poland and Ukraine, and am desperate for the team to stay in Russia. I have a saying that football is life and life is just a game. I believe England fans feel the same.'

The only downside to this love-in was – as an England side at last took an international tournament by the scruff of the neck – that so few fans had travelled with them. Many had quite understandably stayed away after witnessing the savage violence unleashed on innocent supporters by Russian so-called ultras in Marseilles at Euro 2016. For others it was the string of shabby performances at international tournaments – most infamously against Iceland in 2016 – that did for them.

So it was left to the England 'lifers', the die-hards who would follow the

Three Lions anywhere, to provide their unfailing support. Swathed in chain mail, the Cross of St George emblazoned over his heart, Dex Marshall is a familiar face to TV viewers as he has followed his beloved England across continents. Yet after hundreds of games, this faithful knight's loyalty to the Three Lions had been stretched to breaking point following a string of dismal tournament performances.

'I'd had enough,' the financial services worker insisted. 'I felt the team had become disconnected with the supporters. It wasn't just that they were losing; it was the way they were losing.' So, after travelling with England since 1999 from the then war-torn Macedonia to remote Kazakhstan, South Africa and Brazil, he had given Euro 2016 – and the trauma of the Iceland game – a miss. 'But the Gareth Southgate revolution brought me back,' Dex, 58, who now lives in Shanghai, said after England knocked out Colombia on penalties. 'They're young and fearless but down-to-earth. I'm so proud of them.'

Fellow knight Miles Rudham, 51, a businessman from Cobham, Surrey,

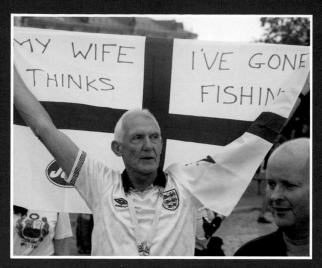

added: 'I'd had enough after Brazil. I flew all the way there for the third game against Costa Rica and we'd already been knocked out of the World Cup by the time I arrived. In my opinion, the players then didn't come over and applaud us enough for making all the effort to get there. This World Cup has restored my faith in the England team, and Russia has welcomed us with open arms.'

Usually the party that follows England fans around – and the sheer numbers of them – is one of the most noticeable features of an international tournament. Reporters covering World Cups have got to know many in this 'family' of football travellers. The core travelling support are not the mindless, plastic-chair-throwing yobs in the imagination of some. Many plan their trips to far-flung destinations around a game, taking in museums and local cuisine, and making new friends along the way.

With his 'Nobby on Tour' flag draped around his shoulders as he strolls through Red Square, Nottingham Forest fan Stuart 'Nobby' Clarke, 60, said: 'I started following England

when my wife Gail died in 2003. You can travel alone and meet up with friends you met at the last game or make new ones. There's a real camaraderie. There aren't many England fans over here, but the ones who made it have been rewarded with a brilliant World Cup.'

Trumpet player with the England band John Hemmingham, 55, said: 'It's like a big family. We all know each other and look out for each other. This time I think people have been put off by the violence they witnessed in Marseilles. They didn't think they'd be able to safely walk around with their flags and England shirts. In fact, the opposite is true. Russians have been so welcoming and friendly. They love British football and culture.'

The dozens of St George flags at games reveal that fans come from football teams the length and breadth of England – from Newcastle to Plymouth, Norwich to Shrewsbury. Essex pub landlord Adam Crane, 40, a veteran of 228 England games, has been to every European nation except for Armenia and the Faroe Islands while

following the team. The dad of three has taken the opportunity to visit Abkhazia, a disputed enclave of Georgia during his World Cup stay. The MK Dons fan said: 'I always do so much more than just go to the game. The expectations were so low this time that few have come. We've been bowled over by how friendly the Russian people are.'

England super-fan Brian Wright, 48, has blown over £100,000 following England over land and sea to more than 340 games. From the temples of Japan to the wilds of Kazakhstan, and taking in South Africa, Belarus and Brazil, he's been tear-gassed, braved ultras – and had to sit through the infamous Iceland defeat. So he's as qualified as anyone to gauge just how good this new-look England are. The football referee, 48, insisted: 'After Iceland there were zero expectations. Now we've finally got a young, fearless team who really want to play for England. It means so much to us long-suffering fans. Football has come home.'

MEANWHILE...
QUARTER-FINAL EXITS

Roberto Martínez said he was the 'proudest man on earth' after his **BELGIUM** stars stunned five-time champions **BRAZIL** in the last eight. Belgium's Golden Generation – criticised for falling short at the 2014 World Cup and Euro 2016 – came of age with a superb 2–1 victory. A Fernandinho own goal and a thumping long-range strike from Manchester City midfielder Kevin De Bruyne rocked Brazil in the first half, and, despite a Renato Augusto goal 14 minutes from time, Belgium held on to reach the semi-finals. This set up a mouthwatering 'derby' against **FRANCE**, with all four semi-finalists coming from Europe.

Spaniard Martinez said: 'The players have done something special and I hope everyone in Belgium is very, very proud. It is a memory we should treasure.' The former Wigan and Everton coach added: 'The way the players believed until the last second was incredible. Brazil have so much finesse and you know they can cut you open. But I didn't think for a second that the players would give up.'

Brazil's departure meant that, after early exits for Lionel Messi and Cristiano Ronaldo, the last of the World Cup's three biggest superstars, Neymar, was also on his way home. Many fans worldwide weren't sad to see him go, though, after his play-acting and theatrics had overshadowed his performances throughout the tournament. After Brazil's last-16 win, Mexico coach Juan Carlos Osorio had slammed Neymar's antics as 'a shame for football' and 'a charade'.

URUGUAY suffered a major setback before their defeat by France when striker Edinson Cavani, two-goal hero of their victory over Portugal, was ruled out with a hamstring injury, and it proved a match to forget for goalkeeper Fernando Muslera. Real Madrid defender Raphaël Varane headed France into the lead shortly before half-time, but the tie was still in the balance until a shocking blunder by Muslera gifted Les Bleus the killer second goal after 61 minutes. There seemed little danger when Antoine Griezmann tried his luck with a speculative 30-yard shot, but the Uruguay keeper horribly misjudged the flight of the ball and could only watch in horror as his weak attempt to palm the ball out saw it loop behind him into the net.

URUGUAY OUT!

On the other side of the draw, ENGLAND's victory over SWEDEN meant Three Lions' fans were able to sit back and relax as they watched prospective semi-finals opponents CROATIA and RUSSIA slug it out in the last of the quarter-finals. For the second successive match, the Croats were taken all the way to penalties, and again it was ice-cool Barcelona star Ivan Rakitić who scored the decisive spot-kick after the match finished 2–2.

It meant the end of the road for hosts Russia's unlikely run into the latter stages, but boss Stanislav Cherchesov said: 'We could only prove our worth by working hard. I believe that people not only started trusting us, but they fell in love with us. The entire country is in love with us.' Croatia boss Zlatko Dalić admitted they were 'lucky' but warned England: 'We are very motivated. We are giving our all. This wasn't a beautiful game, it was a fight, a battle for the semi-final. It will be a battle again, but I trust us, I have belief in us.'

RUSSIA OUT!

'I spoke to the lads before the game and none of us fancied going home,' said Gareth Southgate. England were in a World Cup semi-final. Seventeen of the 23-man squad were not born in 1990, the last time we got this far. One of them, 25-year-old Harry Maguire, posted a picture with girlfriend Fern Hawkins in the stands and wrote: 'Can you ask the neighbours to put the bins out on Monday? We're not going home just yet.'

Skinner and Baddiel's Euro 96 song 'Three Lions', with its iconic chorus, had shot back to No. 1 in the UK charts. But despite 'Football's Coming Home' being sung in nearly every house, car and pub in England, talk of 1966-style glory was tentative in the Three Lions camp. The opponent this time would be a formidable Croatian side, led by the inspired Real Madrid midfielder Luka Modrić.

Dele Alli said: 'It's weird. We are in a bubble at the training camp, coming back, and then getting ready for the next game. It's not until you look at social media you realise how big it is. We know we are in the semi-final, but we are so focused on the games you forget what we have done so far.'

At home, even FA President Prince William was swept up in the excitement. His tweet, from the Kensington Palace account, said: 'You wanted to make history, England, and you are doing just that. This has been an incredible World Cup run and we've enjoyed every minute. You deserve this moment – Football's Coming Home! – W.' Football royalty also backed the team. Sir Geoff Hurst, hat-trick hero of 1966, said: 'We can go all the way – no question.'

Southgate, who joined Sir Alf Ramsey and Sir Bobby Robson as the only England gaffers to reach this stage of the tournament, poured cold water on plans to throw an open-top bus parade for the team no matter what the outcome of the semi-final. He said he would only celebrate a win. Ashley Young added: 'We haven't won anything yet, so there's no point in celebrating.' Eric Dier said: 'I don't think we have succeeded yet. In my eyes, and everyone's back at the hotel, this isn't success yet. We're hungry for more.'

The hopes and dreams of a nation rested on the Lions' shoulders, but the atmosphere in the training camp seemed happy and relaxed. Harry Kane posed for pictures in the hotel sauna, Harry Maguire and goalkeeper Jordan Pickford relaxed in the pool. The team were even pictured larking about with toy chickens on the eve of the match. They played a game of tag in training, which involved chucking the rubber birds to one another. Ashley Young celebrated his 33rd birthday and returned from breakfast to find his room filled with birthday cards and balloons. The team were calm but quietly jubilant.

On the day of the landmark showdown with Croatia, a Boeing 737 crammed full of players, backroom staff and kit flew over to Moscow. The team reportedly got fired up before the game by listening to 80s and 90s tunes in their battle bus on the way to the stadium. Like in the classic New Order footie anthem, the world was in motion. This tournament had surpassed expectations – and so had the England team.

Whatever happened next, the boys had done the nation proud.

SEMI-FINALS

WEDNESDAY

10

JULY

Croatia 2–1 England

Perišić 68   Trippier 5

Mandžukić 109

The nation was still basking in a heatwave and England were one match away from their first major tournament final since 1966. It was already a summer we would never forget. The country ground to a halt at 7pm on Wednesday 11 July, pleading with the Three Lions to make that final push into the history books. But just a few hours later, the dream was over.

Kieran Trippier's stunning free-kick after only five minutes saw wild celebrations around England, with pints of beer hurled into the blue evening sky and strangers hugging each other. But the Three Lions failed to finish off Croatia, who hit back to win 2–1 in extra time.

Captain Harry Kane admitted England were 'gutted' after their unexpected, uplifting World Cup journey ended in heartbreak. He said: 'It's been an amazing run, but it hurts to lose. We wanted to win it and we thought we had enough to go through, but it wasn't to be. In big games, small margins make the difference. There were a few chances after we went 1–0 up and we were on top. That was the time to get another one. It was a 50–50 game after that and unfortunately they got a couple of goals in the big moments. I'm sure we'll look back and there is stuff we should have done, but we worked as hard as we could.

'To get this far and get so close is going to hurt for a while, but we can hold our heads up high. We went further than anyone thought we would. The aim is to make sure England don't have to wait 28 years until our next World Cup semi-final. Hopefully in four years we can go one step further. Two years ago we were in a bad place after Euro 2016, so to pick the nation up and make them feel proud of us again is a big feeling for us.'

With a Final place up for grabs against France – who had edged out Belgium 1–0 the previous night – manager Gareth Southgate named an unchanged team for the third match in succession, while Croatia coach Zlatko Dalić made only one change from the XI who started the quarter-final win over hosts Russia, with Marcelo Brozović in for Andrej Kramarić.

England started confidently and led after only five minutes. Jesse Lingard produced a brilliant piece of skill on the right, beating his man with a cute drag-back and finding Dele Alli, whose surge towards the box was halted by Luka Modrić's clumsy challenge. Turkish referee Cüneyt Çakır awarded a free-kick on the edge of the box, and Trippier stepped up to curl a wonderful shot over the wall and into the top corner. It was his first goal for England.

The Three Lions were playing with a swagger and, from the second of two corners in quick succession, Harry Maguire's downward header went just wide. Croatia did manage a couple of attacks, and after 19 minutes Ivan Perišić went close from outside the area.

But England were looking the most likely, with Raheem Sterling's pace causing panic for defenders Dejan Lovren and Domagoj Vida. Somehow, Lovren escaped a yellow card despite two cynical challenges on Kane and Sterling to stop England attacks.

On the half-hour, England missed a golden chance to make it 2–0 when Lingard's pass put Kane clear. Subašić blocked his sidefooted shot, but the ball broke back to Kane inside the six-yard box and, with Subašić stranded, he looked certain to score. But his effort from a tight angle hit the foot of the post, rebounded on to the keeper and flew across the face of goal to safety. Although the offside flag then went up, replays showed Kane was onside, so the goal would have stood if it had gone to VAR.

England needed a superb last-ditch tackle by Young to thwart Ante Rebić, but they responded with another good move involving Kane and Alli that ended with Lingard guiding a low shot wide when he should have done better.

The momentum shifted drastically after the break. Croatia had clearly rethought their tactics and steadily took control, pressing high up the pitch and giving the likes of John Stones and Jordan Henderson less time to start passing moves from deep.

The first near-miss of the half actually came for England, with Lovren getting a foot in after 56 minutes as Kane tried to meet a Trippier cross with a diving header. But it was no surprise when Croatia, with Luka Modrić and Ivan Rakitić dominating in midfield, got the equaliser. After 68 minutes, Šime Vrsaljko whipped over a cross from the right and Kyle Walker, stooping to clear, was caught out as the flying Perišić lifted his foot above the defender's head to stab the ball into the goal on the volley.

England were wobbling and had a let-off when Stones shanked a clearance to Perišić, who saw his angled shot hit the inside of the post. The Three Lions, who now had Marcus Rashford on for Sterling, did manage a couple of attacks, a Lingard shot skidding wide and Henderson firing a volley well over. But Croatia had two great late chances at the other end. Mario Mandžukić forced Pickford to parry his shot on the turn and, when the England keeper fluffed a punch, Perišić's chip sailed over.

In extra-time England regained some control, but although Croatia had gone to penalties in both previous games, it was Southgate's players who looked tired. With Danny Rose already on for Young, Dier came

'TO GET THIS FAR AND GET SO CLOSE IS GOING TO HURT FOR A WHILE, BUT WE CAN HOLD OUR HEADS UP HIGH. WE WENT FURTHER THAN ANYONE THOUGHT WE WOULD.'

HARRY KANE

KIERAN TRIPPIER'S STUNNING FREE-
KICK AFTER ONLY FIVE MINUTES SAW
WILD CELEBRATIONS AROUND ENGLAND,
WITH PINTS OF BEER HURLED INTO THE
BLUE EVENING SKY AND STRANGERS
HUGGING EACH OTHER.

on for Henderson seven minutes into extra time. Dier was immediately involved, his shot from distance deflecting for a corner. Stones met Trippier's delivery with a powerful header, but Vrsaljko cleared off the line. In added time, Mandžukić was teed up on the edge of the six-yard box by a superb Perišić cross, but Pickford managed to deflect his shot for a corner as the pair collided.

There was no let-off after 109 minutes, however, as Mandžukić scored what proved to be the winner. Trippier, struggling with a groin injury, did not jump to challenge Perišić for a high ball and his header fell to the Juventus striker, who, reacting quicker than Stones, slammed an angled shot past Pickford.

Southgate sent on Jamie Vardy for Walker – only for Trippier to limp off. That left England with ten men for the last few minutes and they never really threatened an equaliser. After Croatia comfortably repelled a last-ditch free-kick from Rashford, the final whistle blew and the England players slumped to the ground, many of them in tears.

There were emotional scenes as the players embraced friends and family in the stands after the game, and the estimated 8,000 England fans at the Luzhniki Stadium stayed behind for an hour, applauding and singing for their beaten heroes.

Boss Southgate said: 'We needed that second goal earlier in the game. In the first half, we were really good and we maybe could have got another goal. We had chances. There was a spell in the second half when their tails were really up, and we had to weather the storm and lost our way a little bit. There was a period when it looked like, "We have the lead and don't want to give it away" rather than "We keep playing". Against the top teams they are the moments in which you continue to play and you keep being brave. We just lost a bit of composure.

'The dressing room is a difficult place. We have just lost a massive game and we all feel the pain of defeat. Did we think we would be in this position? I don't think any of us did. Go back 18 months and no one would have expected us to be in a semi-final of the World Cup. But once you're here and have played as well as we did, you want to take those opportunities in life. We had an opportunity to do what only one team from our nation has ever done and get to a Final.

'But I'm remarkably proud. By the end, several players were out on their feet. The reaction of the fans shows you everything they have given. We have come an incredibly long way in a short space of time. People may have had a feeling that playing for England was always misery and regret and recrimination. Now, I think they have seen it can be enjoyable.'

'IT WASN'T MEANT TO BE. TONIGHT SHOWS HOW FAR WE HAVE COME AS A TEAM AND A NATION. WE HAVE CONNECTED WITH THE FANS AND I HOPE THEY KNOW HOW HARD WE TRIED TO MAKE THEM PROUD.'

KIERAN TRIPPIER

Goal hero Trippier said: 'Obviously we are disappointed, but we have grown as a team through the tournament and handled certain games and a penalty shoot-out well. It wasn't meant to be. Tonight shows how far we have come as a team and a nation. We have connected with the fans and I hope they know how hard we tried to make them proud.'

Walker admitted the players felt that, when Trippier scored, 'it was written in the stars for you to go to the Final and hopefully do something special'. And despite the disappointment, he was lifted by the reception from the fans at the end. He said: 'I was there in France, in the Iceland game, and it was completely different to that. For them to still be singing and chanting our names and singing the manager's name is different.'

Croatia coach Dalić said his tactics 'nullified' England's supply line from Stones and Henderson, and defender Vrsalkjo claimed: 'The all-round perception was that this is a new-look England who have changed their ways of punting long balls upfield, but when we pressed them it turned out that they haven't.'

Captain Modrić said they were fired up by predictions in England that Croatia would be tired after their previous matches and that the Three Lions would be too strong. He said: 'People underestimated Croatia, and that was a huge mistake. All these words from them – we were reading and we were saying, "Okay, today we will see who will be tired." They should be more humble and respect their opponents more. We dominated mentally and physically.'

ENGLAND V CROATIA

ROAROMETER: England goal: 175dB – Howitzer
Defeat: 10dB – Pin dropping

FOOTBALL TO HOME:
1,830 miles (2,945km)

V

🐦 **@JKCorden**
One day, it will come home.
And it will feel incredible. x

🐦 **@liamgallagher**
That England team were biblical and the best thing to come out of this is that we got a proper manager Gareth Southgate you rule LG x

ENGLAND'S biggest game in 28 years – and our best chance of reaching the World Cup Final since 66. The Germans were already home, after all! Around 26.6 million watched at home on ITV – the biggest audience yet – with millions more glued to big screens in public spaces or TVs in pubs and bars.

In London's Hyde Park and at fan parks across the country, roars greeted Kieran Trippier's fifth-minute opener – but there were groans an hour later at Perisic's equaliser, then howls of pain at Mandžukić's extra-time winner. England were out, and in the ITV studio pundits Roy Keane and Ian Wright had a barney – the Irishman claimed England had been planning the victory parade already. Wrighty asked what was wrong with being excited by this young and promising side?

The 45 per cent extra Champagne England fans had bought at Waitrose stayed on ice. And World Cup parties ended with kids in tears as their new heroes failed heroically. Three Lions' fans had spent £264 million on World Cup merchandise, the Centre for Retail Research revealed. England's retro 1980s-style training shirt sold out – despite the £47.95 price tag. And sales of Gareth Southgate's dapper £65 Marks & Spencer waistcoat surged 35 per cent. But don't throw out the flags – the good news is that with Gareth guiding his team of battle-hardened young lions, it could get even better in Qatar in four years' time.

Russia 2018

CHO HYUN-WOO
South Korea

South Korea goalkeeper's caramel-coloured layered look was compared to an ice cream on a cone. He helped boot out Germany, so we forgive him. The difference between success and failure is wafer thin.

1

DOMAGOJ VIDA
Croatia

Receding at the temples, a bad side fade and an apology for a ponytail up top . . . what's not to dislike? Apart from the mousey colour.

2

MILE JEDINAK
Australia

A definite attempt to scare the opposition with a wild-man look, the Aussie actually looked like a jungle-dwelling OAP. Maybe that's why two goalkeepers took pity and let his penalties in.

3

SERGIO RAMOS
Spain

Went to extremes with a skinhead with an even shorter cut around the ears. Didn't help.

4

WILLIAM TROOST-EKONG
Nigeria

Sported a green stripe in his hair to match his Nigeria shirt . . . should have concentrated on earning his stripes on the pitch.

5

DIEGO LAXALT
Uruguay

It's hard not to see Diego and think of Bo Derek running down the beach in the 1979 rom-com 10. Braids are so yesterday . . . and so are Uruguay.

6

Bad Hair XI

7

ANÍBAL GODOY
Panama

Mister T? Nope. Mister E – as in, it's a mystery how he thought this dodgy A-Team style teamed with angular beard was a cool cut.

8

AXEL WITSEL
Belgium

In his Pringle golf sweater-style shirt and bowl-shaped afro, Belgium's water carrier looks like a Jackson Five tribute act on a pro-celeb golf day.

9

RAMIN REZAEIAN
Iran

The swarthy 28-year-old sported a cross between Travis Bickle *Taxi Driver* mohawk and sumptuous Elvis quiff. Neither here nor there . . . a bit like Iran's World Cup.

10

NEYMAR
Brazil

He had more hairdos than goals at Russia 2018. The blond bird's nest must have got in the way of his rolling on the turf. He cut it out – the blond hair, not the rolling.

11

LUKA MODRIĆ
Croatia

Luka to his barber: 'It's just so limp and lifeless. I just don't know what to do with it. Any ideas?' Barber: 'An Alice band?' Get a new barber, Luka. (And no, this isn't sour grapes.)

MANAGER

CARLOS VALDERRAMA
Colombia

Yes, we know he last played for Colombia in 1998 but the 56-year-old striker sported exactly the same shaggy-poodle look 20 years later as he watched his countrymen lose to England.

Fabian Delph had a unique perspective. Having flown home for the birth of his third daughter mid-tournament, he had witnessed the effect that England's astonishing, uplifting World Cup was having on the public. Yes, Croatia had beaten us in the semi-final, leaving just a play-off match for third place, which many thought meaningless, but there were huge positives to take away from Russia.

Delph, on the bench for the Croatia game, said: 'We are role models. I did think we would go back as superheroes, because I genuinely thought we were going to win the World Cup. That has not happened. The four days I did get to go back, I felt the love and support of the nation. It has been great back home – so we need to continue that, to help the young guys look up to us and try to do what we have done. The diversity in the squad has brought people together. It is great for the country, and great for us as players to be part of that and almost force that to happen. Having everyone behind us gave us the push to do as well as we have.'

After the loss in Moscow, Gareth Southgate addressed the squad in the dressing room. He admitted the mood was 'desolate'. Skipper Harry Kane said: 'The gaffer told us

we should be proud of ourselves. We can hold our heads up high. To hear the fans singing out there after a defeat is an incredible feeling. This has to be the start of something rather than the end of it. It is massive that we have had a good tournament, restored the pride of the nation. The fans are excited to watch us again. We are proud of each other. We gave it everything.'

Kane said he hoped to be in the team against Belgium in the play-off, adding: 'It is not a game we wanted to be in. It is what it is, and we will try to play with as much pride as we can and finish on a high.' Asked if he would watch Sunday's final, he said: 'We will probably keep an eye on the score, but I am not too fussed. I will send a good luck message to Hugo Lloris – he is a good friend of mine.'

Fellow Spurs star Danny Rose was upbeat, saying: 'We have to try and kick on – the aim is to win the Euros. We were looking forward to hopefully playing France in the final. We were not scared of France. It is a shame we won't be there.'

Back home, Three Lions' fans were full of praise. Prince William tweeted: 'I couldn't be more proud of this team. You've had an incredible World Cup, made history, and gave us fans something to believe in. We know there is more to come.'

Delph, now a dad of three, put everything into perspective. He said: 'I would hope we are going back to a better country – the nation seems to have been brought together. If we continue to do what we are doing and to unite people, then I am sure we will be living in a better England.'

THIRD-PLACE PLAY-OFF

SATURDAY
14
JULY

Belgium 2–0 England

Meunier 4

Hazard 82

Gareth Southgate said he was 'immensely proud' of his England heroes – even though they couldn't finish their World Cup on a winning note. Goals from Thomas Meunier and Eden Hazard gave Belgium a 2–0 victory in the third-place play-off match in St Petersburg. It meant England couldn't go one better than Bobby Robson's 1990 team, who also finished fourth, or match the third-place finish at the 1968 Euros under Sir Alf Ramsey.

But manager Southgate said: 'Today was always going to be difficult. We played one of the best teams in the world with incredible individual talent, and we had only two days to get ready. I thought it was important to tell the players how proud I was and to recognise how far they got. We were 20 minutes from a World Cup Final three nights ago. The players will have learned a lot in victory and in defeat. Now we look to the future.

'Although we can talk about having a more comfortable route to the semi-final – and, for sure, we did – we have had those routes in the past and not got to the point we have. I'm immensely proud of all the players. And they should be proud of themselves because they have

'I THOUGHT IT WAS IMPORTANT TO TELL THE PLAYERS HOW PROUD I WAS AND TO RECOGNISE HOW FAR THEY GOT.'

GARETH SOUTHGATE

achieved an equal high in terms of tournament performance that any English team that's had to come abroad for a tournament has achieved.'

Southgate had admitted before the game that it had been an 'emotion-filled few days' in the England camp since the heart-breaking semi-final defeat by Croatia, and that his starting XI would reflect the need to 're-energise' the team.

Although the third-place match is derided by many, Southgate promised to take it seriously and his team selection reflected that, with first-choice stars Harry Kane, Raheem Sterling, Jordan Pickford, Kieran Trippier, John Stones and Harry Maguire all in the starting XI. Jordan Henderson, Jesse Lingard, Ashley Young, Kyle Walker and Dele Alli dropped out. In came Phil Jones, Eric Dier, Fabian Delph, Ruben Loftus-Cheek and Danny Rose.

Belgium also fielded a strong team, with key men Eden Hazard and Kevin De Bruyne both included. Manchester United striker Romelu Lukaku – who had an outside chance of knocking Kane off the top of the Golden Boot chart – also started.

The England manager had urged his side to take home bronze medals as proof they had achieved 'something special' at the tournament, but the Three Lions made a sluggish start and fell behind after only four minutes. Belgium were allowed too much time and space to work their way into the final third, and when Nacer Chadli fired in a dangerous cross, Meunier reacted quicker than Rose, getting ahead of him to stab a first-time strike past Pickford.

With Belgium hitting their stride from the first whistle, England were looking vulnerable at the back and Pickford had to turn away a deflected strike from De Bruyne after 11 minutes. The Three Lions shook off their early lethargy and managed a strike on goal after 14 minutes, although goalkeeper Thibaut Courtois comfortably dealt with Delph's long-range effort. Courtois was also untroubled by a Loftus-Cheek header from a Trippier cross, and when Maguire leapt to meet a corner soon afterwards.

After 22 minutes, though, England should have been level. Sterling received the ball on the edge of the box and perfectly teed up Kane, but the captain's trademark clinical finishing deserted him as he screwed his shot wide. That was the last clear-cut chance of the half, and Belgium went in with a deserved 1–0 lead.

With Southgate bringing on Lingard and Marcus Rashford at half-time for Rose and Sterling, England made a brighter start to the second half, but Belgium remained a danger on the counter-attack. Stones was yellow-carded for hauling back Hazard in the centre circle after 52 minutes as the Red Devils' captain threatened to launch a dangerous raid into the England half.

The introduction of Lingard added a new spark to England as an attacking force and he flashed a cross across the face of goal after 54 minutes, with Kane unable to get a touch. Belgium responded by cutting open the England defence again, Lukaku's poor touch allowing Pickford to save at his feet after De Bruyne's delightful pass sent him clear. That was the striker's last meaningful contribution, with Dries Mertens replacing him soon afterwards.

England were turning the screw now and carved out several half-chances. Kane miscued a volley from the edge of the box after a Trippier corner and was then unable to get on the end of a Loftus-Cheek cross that fizzed across the Belgian six-yard area. As England pressed for an equaliser, Dier was getting further forward and, after 69 minutes, he tried his luck with a long-range strike, which Courtois easily saved.

A minute later, Dier did get the better of Courtois, racing through on goal after a one–two with Rashford. Dier looked certain to score as he deftly dinked the ball over the advancing goalkeeper, but his effort didn't have enough pace on it and Toby Alderweireld scrambled back to clear off the line. Dier came close again after 73 minutes, heading wide from eight yards from a Lingard cross, and then Maguire saw his header from a Trippier free-kick drift wide.

It was a familiar tale for England, failing to find the killer touch to turn a period of dominance into goals, and Belgium almost made them pay after 80 minutes when a sweeping passing move from one end of the pitch to the other ended with Mertens crossing to Meunier at the far post. He met the ball with a first-time volley, but Pickford produced an excellent diving save.

The Three Lions survived that scare, but two minutes later Belgium killed them off with another lightning counter-attack. England were committing more and more players forward and were caught short as De Bruyne exploited the space to play in Hazard. He got in front of Jones and coolly tucked the ball inside Pickford's near post.

The goal clearly deflated Southgate's men after their sustained period of dominance, and Belgium were able to see out the game with no further alarms. Losing another match in which they had their share of chances was another harsh lesson, and Southgate conceded: 'We have finished in the final four, but we're not a top-four team yet. Against the very best teams, we have come up short. But we've had a wonderful adventure and some experiences which will stand this group of players and staff in good stead for the future.

'WE HAVE PUT A LOT INTO THE LAST TWO YEARS TO GET TO THIS POINT. THERE WERE SO MANY BRIDGES THAT NEEDED TO BE REBUILT AFTER THE EUROS, AND WE HAVE MANAGED TO DO THINGS THAT ENGLAND TEAMS HAVEN'T DONE FOR A LONG TIME. SO WE'RE PROUD OF THAT.'

ERIC DIER

'We have to try to constantly evolve and improve. We have done that, particularly over the last eight months, and we've had a brilliant adventure here. Every member of our party has enjoyed it immensely. We're very realistic about the level we are. We've had a lot of praise, which has been nice, but we've also balanced that with a lot of reality as well. We don't kid ourselves at all. We know exactly the areas where we hope to get better.

'We're not in club football, where we have a cheque book to buy new players. We have to coach and develop, and the players need a willingness to learn and improve. They have shown that in the last seven weeks. It's nice to have reached a semi-final because that builds belief and gives momentum. There is some evidence that they can have success, and they can feel that and commit to the England shirt. But we need to keep improving.'

Southgate singled out Stones as 'outstanding' against Belgium and goalkeeper Pickford for his 'wonderful tournament'. Captain Kane, England's talisman earlier in the campaign, was again largely ineffective against Belgium, and the way his influence faded as the tournament progressed had led to speculation that he was carrying an injury. Southgate said: 'Today is the seventh game in a short period of time and we have had incredible physical and emotional demands in the tournament. It would be wrong to judge any player on today's game if their energy levels were short. I think Harry has captained the team exceptionally well.'

Kane said: 'I thought we played really well in the second half. We had them on the ropes, but we couldn't get the goal. I can't fault the lads. We gave it everything. Today shows there's still room for improvement. We've said that all along.' On the prospect of him winning the Golden Boot thanks to his six goals in the first four games, he added: 'It shows we had a very good group stage and scored a lot of goals. Obviously, I'm disappointed I couldn't get a goal in the last few games, but sometimes it goes for you, sometimes it doesn't. If I get the Golden Boot, it will be something I'll be very proud of.'

His Tottenham team-mate Dier, reflecting on the tournament, said: 'We have put a lot into the last two years to get to this point. There were so many bridges that needed to be rebuilt after the Euros, and we have managed to do things that England teams haven't done for a long time. So we're proud of that. There's still a lot of work to be done to improve as a collective and as individuals. But it's been a fantastic experience and one we'll remember.'

'WE GAVE IT EVERYTHING.
TODAY SHOWS THERE'S
STILL ROOM FOR
IMPROVEMENT.'

THIRD-PLACE PLAY-OFF

FOOTBALL TO HOME:
1,785 miles (2,874 km)

V

🐦 @HKane
Not the way we wanted to finish but so many positives to take from this experience. Travelling fans and everyone back home have been great – thank you. #ENG #ThreeLions #WorldCup

Many of the big screens were already down. The pain of brave defeat was fresh. And the final was the following day. So only half of us came home to watch the bronze-medal match on ITV. Around 5.3 million saw the whole game – another 3 million had a sneaky peek to check the score – as England were beaten for the second time in the tournament by Belgium (who may have wished they hadn't won the first match to earn a tougher route to the final).

In Newcastle, tickets for a showing in Times Square were free but only a handful turned out. If our exit was a turn OFF for the nation, at least our performances had turned ON half the nation. Thirty per cent of women reported England's thrilling World Cup ride had made them more frisky, according to a poll. Population experts predicted 5,000 extra births for next March – so by the 2038 tournament we could have even more great young players to choose from.

The only winners after England's third defeat in Russia 2018 were the FA, who earned £16.6 million prize money for our fourth place. In Leeds, council bosses kept the giant screen up in Millennium Square but put Wimbledon tennis on it to save brass, 'following consideration of the resources to manage and facilitate a designated event-type screening', apparently.

But first things first. The next World Cup kicks off on 21 November 2022 in Qatar. So there are just 1,591 more days of hurt before our next bid to bring football – the World Cup – home.

HARRY'S GOLDEN BOOT

	HARRY KANE	ENGLAND	6
	DENIS CHERYSHEV	RUSSIA	4
	ANTOINE GRIEZMANN	FRANCE	4
	ROMELU LUKAKU	BELGIUM	4
	KYLIAN MBAPPÉ	FRANCE	4
	CRISTIANO RONALDO	PORTUGAL	4

When he was six, Harry Kane was stopping goals, not scoring them. At Ridgeway Rovers, the London youth team where David Beckham started out, the trialling youngster volunteered to go between the sticks. Heroics ensued, and Rovers thought they had found their new goalkeeper. But a whisper in the coach's ear said he was better at the other end of the pitch. The gloves came off, the goals went in – and Harry Kane became a striker.

Nineteen years later, the Three Lions captain was top scorer at the World Cup, the only Englishman to have won the Golden Boot other than Gary Lineker in 1986. Lineker, now 57, joked he was glad he finally had some company. Both scored six for their trophy, but it was not a foregone conclusion for 24-year-old Harry in Russia. This was a tournament of thirsty young guns.

An early brace against Tunisia and a hat-trick in the 6–1 rout of Panama ensured Kane was the man to beat. Two of his rivals – Portugal superstar Cristiano Ronaldo and Russia's Denis Cheryshev – were knocked out in the last 16 and quarter-finals respectively, with four goals apiece. But Belgium's Romelu Lukaku and French duo Antoine Griezmann and Kylian Mbappé could all potentially have poached the accolade in their final games.

Kane's treble against Panama comprised two unstoppable penalties and a lucky deflection off the back of his heel. It made him only the third English player to hit a World Cup hat-trick, after Sir Geoff Hurst in the 1966 final against West Germany, and Lineker in a group game against Poland at Mexico 1986.

After so many years of hurt, Kane could have buckled under the pressure of spearheading one of the youngest teams at the tournament. And as the Three Lions' talisman, he was battered by defenders of lesser teams trying to sneak their way to victory. But nothing worked. Against Colombia in the last 16, he was floored by Carlos Sánchez and correctly awarded a penalty. The South Americans shamelessly scuffed the penalty spot while swarming around the referee. It took three minutes for Kane to finally step up, and he duly slotted it home – before repeating the feat in the nail-biting shoot-out that followed.

Kane didn't score again in the tournament but those six goals were enough for him to join Ronaldo (the Brazilian one), Germany's Miroslav Klose, Italy's Paolo Rossi and Portuguese legend Eusébio on the esteemed list of World Cup Golden Boot winners.

'Not many people get to say they have won a Golden Boot at a World Cup,' said the Tottenham ace, who missed the presentation ceremony after the final as he was already heading home. He added: 'I'm sure they will send it to me in a nice secure package! The Golden Boot will go with the other two, the Premier League ones. It's a big achievement. I wanted to prove to myself I could score at this level. I have scored at every other level and it was important I did that. I am extremely proud. It's been a fantastic campaign for me personally and the team as well. But there is still stuff I can improve on. Obviously, I can get better. I feel like there have been games in this tournament when I could have done better, but that's all part of the learning curve.'

If this isn't Harry Kane at his peak, then we can't wait for Euro 2020 . . .

MEANWHILE...
THE FINAL

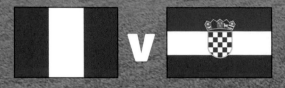

 Didier Deschamps hailed his young French side's 'supreme coronation' after they beat **CROATIA** 4–2 in a dramatic final in Moscow. **FRANCE** claimed their second world title in an incident-packed showdown at the Luzhniki Stadium, the match turning on a controversial penalty awarded using VAR. Croatia, the smallest nation to reach the Final since Uruguay in 1950, dominated the first half and battled back to equalise with a fine 28th-minute strike from Ivan Perišić after Mario Mandžukić's own goal ten minutes earlier had given France the lead against the run of play.

But Argentinian referee Néstor Pitana's decision to penalise Perišić for handball proved pivotal. The big moment came after 34 minutes when the ball struck Perišić on the arm from a corner and, after French protests, the VAR team advised Pitana to review the incident on a pitchside monitor. It took four minutes and 20 seconds from the moment the incident happened to Antoine Griezmann coolly beating goalkeeper Danijel Subašić from the spot.

Paul Pogba's measured shot after 59 minutes put France within touching distance of glory, and 19-year-old Kylian Mbappé scored with an audacious 25-yard effort six minutes later. Croatia were given a lifeline with 21 minutes left when France captain and goalkeeper Hugo Lloris tried to dribble past Mandžukić on the edge of his six-yard area and the striker poked the ball home. However, France comfortably saw out the closing stages.

Mbappé's goal made him the first teenager to score in the final since Pelé in 1958, while coach Deschamps became only the third coach after Brazil's Mário Zagallo and Germany's Franz Beckenbauer to win the World Cup as player and coach. Deschamps, whose team suffered a shock defeat by Portugal on home soil in the Euro 2016 final, said: 'Two years ago it was so painful. We did learn a lot from that. We put too much emphasis on that match. We tried to stay relaxed this time.'

There were wild celebrations on the pitch as France received the trophy in the middle of a thunderstorm, and, later, the players invaded Deschamps' press conference, spraying him with champagne. Deschamps said: 'They're completely crazy, those lads! They're young and they're happy. Professionally, there's nothing above this. I had an immense privilege to live through this as a player 20 years ago and it was in France, so it will be marked in my memory forever, but what the players did today is just as beautiful. This is the supreme coronation.'

Croatia coach Zlatko Dalić said: 'In the World Cup Final you do not give such a penalty. When VAR goes in your favour it's good, when it doesn't it's bad. In the first six games we may have been favoured by luck. Today, not.'

Captain Luka Modrić, named player of the tournament, said: 'It's hard when you come so close and fall short. We were the better team for much of the game. Unfortunately, some clumsy goals swung it their way.'

And defender Dejan Lovren claimed: 'France didn't play football. They waited for their chance and scored. They played every game of the tournament like that. We played much better football than them.' But Deschamps hit back: 'Yes, there are imperfections. Today was not perfect. But we did have the mentality and psychological qualities that are decisive. What people will remember is that France is world champion. That means we did things better than the others.'

HEROES AND ZEROES OF THE WORLD CUP

 # Winners!

>> RUSSIA

Labelled the worst team in the tournament by their own fans, Russia smashed five past Saudi Arabia at the Luzhniki Stadium before an ecstatic home crowd, then beat Egypt to reach the second round, where they stunned the world by knocking out 2010 winners Spain on penalties. Terrible game . . . unforgettable party. Croatia eventually stopped them in the quarter-final, but Russia deserved their shock success.

>> MARQUANE FELLAINI

The big-haired bench-warmer at Manchester United had been playing the same role brilliantly for Belgium. But 2-0 down to Japan and heading out, Fellaini went on. His physical presence – and 74th-minute equaliser – changed everything. With seconds to go, Belgium broke away and got the winner. Fellaini's heroics even won the 30-year-old a new two-year contract back on the bench at Old Trafford.

>> VAR

The new Video Assistant Referee technology was the biggest change at this tournament. It was controversial, with games held up as players surrounded the ref to demand a TV review – or begged him not to. On balance, fairness won. Expect playground kickabouts to be full of kids drawing a screen in the air rather than shouting 'Referee!' when they're hacked to the ground.

>> JULEN LOPETEGUI

Spain's manager got the boot two days before the tournament kicked off when news emerged he had agreed to become Real Madrid's new boss. At first it seemed beginner's luck might help stand-in coach Fernando Hierro. Only Cristiano Ronaldo's genius free-kick stopped them winning their first group game. But defeat on penalties by Russia at the first knockout match killed the dream. While former Real Madrid and, yes, Bolton Wanderers star Fernando went from Hierro to zero, Lopetegui not only landed a huge pay rise and a dream job bossing the Champions League winners, but can claim Spain would have won if he'd been left in charge.

>> JAPAN

While their fans filled up their own rubbish bags after matches, the players swept aside Colombia 2–1, drew 2–2 with Senegal and were only narrowly beaten 1–0 by Poland. Then they roared to a shock 2–0 lead against Belgium's Golden Generation – with Takashi Inui scoring one of the goals of the tournament. West Brom's Nacer Chadli hit a 94th-minute winner that broke Japanese hearts but won them admirers around the world. Tidy!

>> CHRIS WADDLE

No longer will the Geordie winger's heartbreaking 1990 semi-final shoot-out miss be the symbol of our World Cup woes. We finally won one, remember! So TV stations can replay Jordan Pickford's blinding one-handed save . . . rather than Waddle's ballooned shot.

>> LINCOLN CITY

England had failed to score from a set-piece at a major tournament for eight years. But manager Gareth Southgate looked to the League Two side's corner tactics to master the art. Dubbed the 'Love Train' by pundit and ex-England boss Glenn Hoddle, players line up closely facing the goal before darting away to either side. And with Harry Kane in the box instead of taking the corners, the goals flowed.

Losers!

» GERMANY

The reigning champions' shock opening-match defeat to Mexico 1–0 was not a blip. Although Toni Kroos's brilliant last-minute free-kick helped them beat Sweden 2–1 in the next match, when they should have kicked on they were kicked out. In their final group match, South Korea inflicted a humiliating 2–0 defeat, making it the Germans' worst World Cup since 1938. Boss Joachim Löw is staying on. But even he must be sniffing the winds of change.

» LIONEL MESSI

This was perhaps the 31-year-old genius's last chance to follow in Maradona's footsteps and land the prize his talents deserve. But it all ended messily. Hapless coach Jorge Sampaoli, goalkeeping clangers and Messi's own missed penalty against Iceland wrecked the side's confidence. Despite his two assists against France, Argentina crashed out 4–3. Now there are calls to drop him. Fed up and frustrated, Messi is likely to quit international football first.

» CRISTIANO RONALDO

Started bang on form with a hat-trick against Spain – including a blinding last-minute free-kick – that earned Portugal a 3–3 draw in a pulsating match. He became the country's first player to score in four World Cups and he hit the winner against Morocco. Then it all went wrong. A penalty miss against Iran was followed by defeat in the second round to Uruguay. Juventus paid Real Madrid £99 million for Ronaldo days later. But the 33-year-old is unlikely to be the same force, even if he does make it to Qatar 2022.

» NEYMAR

With Neymar playing his way to fitness in the opening matches, Brazil were on a roll . . . just like him. Yes, the £198-million Paris Saint-Germain genius was the target of tough tackles, but his constant horizontal theatrics took the team's eye off the ball and everyone's favourite other team were beaten 2–1 in the quarter-finals by Belgium. It wasn't as laughable as the 7–1 defeat to Germany in 2014, but Neymar's antics launched a string of hilarious memes, rolling through space, along roads and even a bowling alley. Strike!

» COLOMBIA

Snarling, snapping, wrestling, whingeing . . . the only thing Colombia didn't do against England was play decent football. With playmaker James Rodríguez injured, the South Americans tried to reduce the second-round clash with England to a brawl. An equaliser in the fourth minute of added time – three minutes of which they won moaning about a stonewall penalty – gave them a reprieve. But Eric Dier's historic shoot-out kick sent them home.

» WILLY CABALLERO

When 36-year-old Manchester City keeper Willy Caballero made his World Cup debut against Iceland in place of injured Sergio Romero, he looked iffy. And in his second match he produced the howler of the tournament, clipping a clearance up perfectly for Croatia's Ante Rebi to volley straight past him. It sparked a 3–0 defeat that rocked Argentina. Wonky Willy was dropped, but the damage was done.

» TIKI-TAKA

The intricate passing game was the key to Spain's first World Cup win in 2010 and the European Championships victories either side of it. But four years ago they were destroyed by Holland. And this time, even peerless Andrés Iniesta – who knitted their tiki-taka football together – couldn't stop them being knocked out by Russia. Ageing Iniesta's international retirement at 34 may mean a fundamental change in Spain's style.

WE'RE COMING HOME

It was very different to the homecoming in 1990, when 200,000 proud fans welcomed the England team back from Italy. Like this time, the Three Lions had reached the semi-finals and lost the third-place play-off. Back then, an open-top bus parade through Luton allowed the nation to show its gratitude to Gazza, Lineker & co. This time, boss Gareth Southgate had asked fans to stay away. He didn't want to send the wrong message to the young squad – that coming fourth was enough.

So, ten minutes before France faced Croatia in the final in Moscow, a charter jet touched down at Birmingham Airport, greeted by 300 loyal supporters who had ignored Southgate's request and cheered from behind barbed-wire fences as the 23-man squad stepped off the plane at a cargo terminal. Skipper and Golden Boot winner Harry Kane looked happy and relaxed. The team posed in tracksuits for a final photo. Raheem Sterling could be seen doing keepy-uppies and Southgate hugged his players.

Jesse Lingard tweeted: 'It's been an amazing journey with a great group of people, we enjoyed every moment through the ups and downs and there is so much more to come from us all. Want to thank everybody that followed us from beginning to end. Different class, thank you.' The players were driven off in a fleet of chauffeured Mercedes past fans lining the streets and hoping for a glimpse. Wing-back Ashley Young was one of the few players to wave as the cars sped past.

Many fans felt it was a shame they were unable to show their appreciation. Karen Dench, 28, said: 'They should have had a better celebration as it is the best performance we've had in 28 years. I think we should have had a parade to let fans come and show their support.' Daran Philipson, 45, said: 'I know Southgate doesn't want a fuss, but I think there should have been some sort of reception. After all, they got to the semi-finals.'

England's understated return was in marked contrast to the tumultuous scenes in Brussels as the Belgium team came home. The players, who beat England in the play-off to claim third place, had an open-top bus ride and an audience with King Philippe and Queen Mathilde. Tens of thousands turned out to cheer.

Back in the UK, Kane tweeted a picture of the squad next to the plane. With one simple message, he spoke for all of England – the players, their families, the thousands of fans in Russia, the millions of fans back home, the kids, the pensioners, even the exhausted pub staff – who had been brought together by this unexpectedly joyous World Cup.

'Loved it, lads,' wrote Harry – with a heart, an England flag and a lion emoji.

RESULTS TABLES

GROUP A

Position	Team	Played	Won	Drawn	Lost	GF	GA	GD	Points
1	URUGUAY	3	3	0	0	5	0	+5	9
2	RUSSIA	3	2	0	1	8	4	+4	6
3	SAUDI ARABIA	3	1	0	2	2	7	-5	3
4	EGYPT	3	0	0	3	2	6	-4	0

14 JUNE 2018, LUZHNIKI STADIUM, MOSCOW

RUSSIA 5 – 0 **SAUDI ARABIA**

Gazinskii 12
Cheryshev 43
Dzyuba 71
Cheryshev 90+1
Golovin 90+4

15 JUNE 2018, CENTRAL STADIUM, YEKATERINBURG

EGYPT 0 – 1 **URUGUAY**

Giménez 89

19 JUNE 2018, KRESTOVSKY STADIUM, SAINT PETERSBURG

RUSSIA 3 – 1 **EGYPT**

Fathy 47 (o.g.)
Cheryshev 59
Dzyuba 62

Salah 73 (pen.)

20 JUNE 2018, ROSTOV ARENA, ROSTOV-ON-DON

URUGUAY 1 – 0 **SAUDI ARABIA**

Suárez 23

25 JUNE 2018, COSMOS ARENA, SAMARA

URUGUAY 3 – 0 **RUSSIA**

Suárez 10
Cheryshev 23 (o.g.)
Cavani 90

25 JUNE 2018, VOLGOGRAD ARENA, VOLGOGRAD

SAUDI ARABIA 2 – 1 **EGYPT**

Al-Faraj 45+6 (pen.)
Al-Dawsari 90+5

Salah 22

GROUP B

Position	Team	Played	Won	Drawn	Lost	GF	GA	GD	Points
1	SPAIN	3	1	2	0	6	5	+1	5
2	PORTUGAL	3	1	2	0	5	4	+1	5
3	IRAN	3	1	1	1	2	2	0	4
4	MOROCCO	3	0	1	2	2	4	-2	1

15 JUNE 2018, KRESTOVSKY STADIUM, SAINT PETERSBURG

MOROCCO 0 – 1 **IRAN**

Bouhaddouz 90+5 (o.g.)

15 JUNE 2018, FISHT OLYMPIC STADIUM, SOCHI

PORTUGAL 3 – 3 **SPAIN**

Ronaldo 4 (pen.)
Ronaldo 44
Ronaldo 88

Costa 24
Costa 55
Nacho 58

20 JUNE 2018, LUZHNIKI STADIUM, MOSCOW

PORTUGAL 1 – 0 **MOROCCO**

Ronaldo 4

20 JUNE 2018, KAZAN ARENA, KAZAN

IRAN 0 – 1 **SPAIN**

Costa 54

25 JUNE 2018, MORDOVIA ARENA, SARANSK

IRAN 1 – 1 **PORTUGAL**

Ansarifard 90+3 (pen.)

Quaresma 45

25 JUNE 2018, KALININGRAD STADIUM, KALININGRAD

SPAIN 2 – 2 **MOROCCO**

Isco 19
Aspas 90+1

Boutaïb 14
En-Nesyri 81

GROUP C

Position	Team	Played	Won	Drawn	Lost	GF	GA	GD	Points
1	FRANCE	3	2	1	0	3	1	+2	7
2	DENMARK	3	1	2	0	2	1	+1	5
3	PERU	3	1	0	2	2	2	0	3
4	AUSTRALIA	3	0	1	2	2	5	-3	1

16 JUNE 2018, KAZAN ARENA, KAZAN

FRANCE 2 – 1 **AUSTRALIA**

Griezmann 58 (pen.)
Behich 81 (o.g.)

Jedinak 62 (pen.)

16 JUNE 2018, MORDOVIA ARENA, SARANSK

PERU 0 – 1 **DENMARK**

Poulsen 59

21 JUNE 2018, COSMOS ARENA, SAMARA

DENMARK 1 – 1 **AUSTRALIA**

Eriksen 7

Jedinak 38 (pen.)

21 JUNE 2018, CENTRAL STADIUM, YEKATERINBURG

FRANCE 1 – 0 **PERU**

Mbappé 34

26 JUNE 2018, LUZHNIKI STADIUM, MOSCOW

DENMARK 0 – 0 **FRANCE**

26 JUNE 2018, FISHT OLYMPIC STADIUM, SOCHI

AUSTRALIA 0 – 2 **PERU**

Carrillo 18
Guerrero 50

GROUP D

Position	Team	Played	Won	Drawn	Lost	GF	GA	GD	Points
1	CROATIA	3	3	0	0	7	1	+6	9
2	ARGENTINA	3	1	1	1	3	5	-2	4
3	NIGERIA	3	1	0	2	3	4	-1	3
4	ICELAND	3	0	1	2	2	5	-3	1

16 JUNE 2018, OTKRITIE ARENA, MOSCOW

ARGENTINA 1 – 1 **ICELAND**

Agüero 19

Finnbogason 23

16 JUNE 2018, KALININGRAD STADIUM, KALININGRAD

CROATIA 2 – 0 **NIGERIA**

Etebo 32 (o.g.)
Modrić 71 (pen.)

21 JUNE 2018, NIZHNY NOVGOROD STADIUM, NIZHNY NOVGOROD

ARGENTINA 0 – 3 **CROATIA**

Rebić 53
Modrić 80
Rakitić 90+1

22 JUNE 2018, VOLGOGRAD ARENA, VOLGOGRAD

NIGERIA 2 – 0 **ICELAND**

Musa 49
Musa 75

26 JUNE 2018, KRESTOVSKY STADIUM, SAINT PETERSBURG

NIGERIA 1 – 2 **ARGENTINA**

Moses 51 (pen.)

Messi 14
Rojo 86

26 JUNE 2018, ROSTOV ARENA, ROSTOV-ON-DON

ICELAND 1 – 2 **CROATIA**

G. Sigurðsson 76 (pen.)

Badelj 53
Perišić 90

GROUP STAGE

GROUP E

Position	Team	Played	Won	Drawn	Lost	GF	GA	GD	Points
1	BRAZIL	3	2	1	0	5	1	+4	7
2	SWITZERLAND	3	1	2	0	5	4	+1	5
3	SERBIA	3	1	0	2	2	4	-2	3
4	COSTA RICA	3	0	1	2	2	5	-3	1

17 JUNE 2018, COSMOS ARENA, SAMARA

COSTA RICA 0 – 1 **SERBIA**

Kolarov 56

17 JUNE 2018, ROSTOV ARENA, ROSTOV-ON-DON

BRAZIL 1 – 1 **SWITZERLAND**

Coutinho 20   Zuber 50

22 JUNE 2018, KRESTOVSKY STADIUM, SAINT PETERSBURG

BRAZIL 2 – 0 **COSTA RICA**

Coutinho 90+1
Neymar 90+7

22 JUNE 2018, KALININGRAD STADIUM, KALININGRAD

SERBIA 1 – 2 **SWITZERLAND**

Mitrović 5   Xhaka 52
                   Shaqiri 90

27 JUNE 2018, OTKRITIE ARENA, MOSCOW

SERBIA 0 – 2 **BRAZIL**

                   Paulinho 36
                   Thiago Silva 68

27 JUNE 2018, NIZHNY NOVGOROD STADIUM, NIZHNY NOVGOROD

SWITZERLAND 2 – 2 **COSTA RICA**

Džemaili 31   Waston 56
Drmić 88   Sommer 90+3 (o.g.)

GROUP F

Position	Team	Played	Won	Drawn	Lost	GF	GA	GD	Points
1	SWEDEN	3	2	0	1	5	2	+3	6
2	MEXICO	3	2	0	1	3	4	-1	6
3	SOUTH KOREA	3	1	0	2	3	3	0	3
4	GERMANY	3	1	0	2	2	4	-2	3

17 JUNE 2018, LUZHNIKI STADIUM, MOSCOW

GERMANY 0 – 1 **MEXICO**

Lozano 35

18 JUNE 2018, NIZHNY NOVGOROD STADIUM, NIZHNY NOVGOROD

SWEDEN 1 – 0 **SOUTH KOREA**

Granqvist 65 (pen.)

23 JUNE 2018, ROSTOV ARENA, ROSTOV-ON-DON

SOUTH KOREA 1 – 2 **MEXICO**

Son Heung-min   Vela 26 (pen.)
90+3   Hernández 66

23 JUNE 2018, FISHT OLYMPIC STADIUM, SOCHI

GERMANY 2 – 1 **SWEDEN**

Reus 48   Toivonen 32
Kroos 90+5

27 JUNE 2018, KAZAN ARENA, KAZAN

SOUTH KOREA 2 – 0 **GERMANY**

Kim Young-gwon
90+3
Son Heung-min
90+6

27 JUNE 2018, CENTRAL STADIUM, YEKATERINBURG

MEXICO 0 – 3 **SWEDEN**

                   Augustinsson 50
                   Granqvist 62 (pen.)
                   Álvarez 74 (o.g.)

GROUP G

Position	Team	Played	Won	Drawn	Lost	GF	GA	GD	Points
1	BELGIUM	3	3	0	0	9	2	+7	9
2	ENGLAND	3	2	0	1	8	3	+5	6
3	TUNISIA	3	1	0	2	5	8	-3	3
4	PANAMA	3	0	0	3	2	11	-9	0

JUNE 2018, FISHT OLYMPIC STADIUM, SOCHI

BELGIUM 3 – 0 **PANAMA**

Mertens 47
Lukaku 69
Lukaku 75

18 JUNE 2018, VOLGOGRAD ARENA, VOLGOGRAD

TUNISIA 1 – 2 **ENGLAND**

Sassi 35 (pen.)   Kane 11
                     Kane 90+1

23 JUNE 2018, OTKRITIE ARENA, MOSCOW

BELGIUM 5 – 2 **TUNISIA**

Hazard 6 (pen.)   Bronn 18
Lukaku 16   Khazri 90+3
Lukaku 45+3
E. Hazard 51
Batshuayi 90

24 JUNE 2018, NIZHNY NOVGOROD STADIUM, NIZHNY NOVGOROD

ENGLAND 6 – 1 **PANAMA**

Stones 8   Baloy 78
Kane 22 (pen.)
Lingard 36
Stones 40
Kane 45+1 (pen.)
Kane 62

28 JUNE 2018, KALININGRAD STADIUM, KALININGRAD

ENGLAND 0 – 1 **BELGIUM**

Januzaj 51

28 JUNE 2018, MORDOVIA ARENA, SARANSK

PANAMA 1 – 2 **TUNISIA**

Meriah 33 (o.g.)   F. Ben Youssef 51
                     Khazri 66

GROUP H

Position	Team	Played	Won	Drawn	Lost	GF	GA	GD	Points
1	COLOMBIA	3	2	0	1	5	2	+3	6
2	JAPAN	3	1	1	1	4	4	0	4
3	SENEGAL	3	1	1	1	4	4	0	4
4	POLAND	3	1	0	2	2	5	-3	3

19 JUNE 2018, MORDOVIA ARENA, SARANSK

COLOMBIA 1 – 2 **JAPAN**

Quintero 39   Kagawa 6 (pen.)
                     Osako 73

19 JUNE 2018, OTKRITIE ARENA, MOSCOW

POLAND 1 – 2 **SENEGAL**

Krychowiak 86   Cionek 37 (o.g.)
                     Niang 60

24 JUNE 2018, CENTRAL STADIUM, YEKATERINBURG

JAPAN 2 – 2 **SENEGAL**

Inui 34   Mané 11
Honda 78   Wagué 71

24 JUNE 2018, KAZAN ARENA, KAZAN

POLAND 0 – 3 **COLOMBIA**

Mina 40
Falcao 70
Ju. Cuadrado 75

28 JUNE 2018, VOLGOGRAD ARENA, VOLGOGRAD

JAPAN 0 – 1 **POLAND**

Bednarek 59

28 JUNE 2018, COSMOS ARENA, SAMARA

SENEGAL 0 – 1 **COLOMBIA**

Mina 74

ROUND OF 16

30 JUNE 2018, KAZAN ARENA, KAZAN

FRANCE 4 – 3 **ARGENTINA**

Griezmann 13 (pen.)
Pavard 57
Mbappé 64
Mbappé 68

Di María 41
Mercado 48
Agüero 90+3

30 JUNE 2018, FISHT OLYMPIC STADIUM, SOCHI

URUGUAY 2 – 1 **PORTUGAL**

Cavani 7
Cavani 62

Pepe 55

1 JULY 2018, LUZHNIKI STADIUM, MOSCOW

SPAIN 1 – 1 **RUSSIA (A.E.T.)**

Sergei Ignashevich 12 (o.g.)

Dzyuba 41 (pen)

RUSSIA WIN 4–3 ON PENALTIES

1 JULY 2018, NIZHNY NOVGOROD STADIUM, NIZHNY NOVGOROD

CROATIA 1 – 1 **DENMARK (A.E.T.)**

Mandžukić 4

M. Jørgensen 1

CROATIA WIN 3–2 ON PENALTIES

2 JULY 2018, COSMOS ARENA, SAMARA

BRAZIL 2 – 0 **MEXICO**

Neymar 51
Firmino 88

2 JULY 2018, ROSTOV ARENA, ROSTOV-ON-DON

BELGIUM 3 – 2 **JAPAN**

Vertonghen 69
Fellaini 74
Chadli 90+4

Haraguchi 48
Inui 52

3 JULY 2018, KRESTOVSKY STADIUM, SAINT PETERSBURG

SWEDEN 1 – 0 **SWITZERLAND**

Forsberg 66

3 JULY 2018, OTKRITIE ARENA, MOSCOW

COLOMBIA 1 – 1 **ENGLAND (A.E.T.)**

Y. Mina 90+3

Kane 57 (pen.)

ENGLAND WIN 4–3 ON PENALTIES

QUARTER-FINALS

6 JULY 2018, NIZHNY NOVGOROD STADIUM, NIZHNY NOVGOROD

 URUGUAY 0 – 2 **FRANCE**

Varane 40
Griezmann 61

6 JULY 2018, KAZAN ARENA, KAZAN

 BRAZIL 1 – 2 **BELGIUM**

Renato Augusto 76

Fernandinho 13 (o.g.)
De Bruyne 31

7 JULY 2018, COSMOS ARENA, SAMARA

 SWEDEN 0 – 2 **ENGLAND**

Maguire 30
Alli 59

7 JULY 2018, FISHT OLYMPIC STADIUM, SOCHI

 RUSSIA 2 – 2 **CROATIA (A.E.T.)**

Cheryshev 31
Fernandes 115

Kramarić 39
Vida 101

CROATIA WIN 4–3 ON PENALTIES

SEMI-FINALS

10 JULY 2018, KRESTOVSKY STADIUM, SAINT PETERSBURG

 FRANCE 1 – 0 **BELGIUM**

Umtiti 51

RUSSIA WIN 4–3 ON PENALTIES

11 JULY 2018, LUZHNIKI STADIUM, MOSCOW

 CROATIA 2 – 1 **ENGLAND (A.E.T.)**

Perišić 68
Mandžukić 109

Trippier 5

THIRD-PLACE PLAY-OFF

14 JULY 2018, KRESTOVSKY STADIUM, SAINT PETERSBURG

 BELGIUM 2 – 0 **ENGLAND**

Meunier 4
E. Hazard 82

FINAL

15 JULY 2018, LUZHNIKI STADIUM, MOSCOW

 FRANCE 4 – 2 **CROATIA**

Mandžukić 18 (o.g.)
Griezmann 38 (pen.)
Pogba 59
Mbappé 65

Perišić 28
Mandžukić 69

HarperCollins*Publishers*
1 London Bridge Street
London SE1 9GF

www.harpercollins.co.uk

First published by HarperCollins*Publishers* 2018

10 9 8 7 6 5 4 3 2 1

A catalogue record of this book is available from
the British Library

ISBN 978-0-00-832207-6

Design by Louise Leffler

Printed and bound in Great Britain by Bell & Bain Ltd., Glasgow

MIX
Paper from
responsible sources
FSC™ C007454

FSC™ is a non-profit international organisation established to
promote the responsible management of the world's forests.
Products carrying the FSC label are independently certified to
assure consumers that they come from forests that are managed
to meet the social, economic and ecological needs of present
and future generations, and other controlled sources.

Find out more about HarperCollins and the environment at
www.harpercollins.co.uk/green

PICTURE CREDITS

While every effort has been made to trace the owners of copyright
material reproduced herein and secure permissions, the publishers
would like to apologise for any omissions and will be pleased to
incorporate missing acknowledgements in any future edition of
this book.

© Action Images via Reuters/Andrew Couldridge p22; © AFP/Getty
Images p111; © AFP/Getty Images/Martin Bernetti p100; © Alex
Livesey/Getty Images p182; © Alex Morton/Getty Images p40, p106;
© Alexander Demianchuk/TASS via Getty Images p153 (bottom); ©
Allsport Co./Getty Images p173; © Amin Mohammad Jamali/Getty
Images p74; © Angel Martinez/Real Madrid via Getty Images p182;

© Anton Novoderezhkin/TASS via Getty Images p128; © Benjamin
Cremel/AFP/Getty Images p166 (1); © Bob Thomas/Getty Images
p15, p16, p133, p182; © Catherine Ivill/Getty Images p114, p175; ©
Charlotte Graham/AFP/Getty Images p25;
© Chris Brunskill/Fantasista/Getty Images p27, p65, p71, p94,
p120, p182; © Chris J Ratcliffe/Getty Images p149 (bottom); ©
Clive Brunskill/Getty Images p96–7; © Clive Mason/Getty Images
p99; © Clive Rose – FIFA/FIFA via Getty Images p29, p35, p45,
p47, p51, p55, p57, p59, p60, p67, p72; © Clive Rose/Getty Images
p21, p30, p108, p148, p164; © Dan Mullan/Getty Images p18,
p78–9, p166 (4); © Darren Fletcher/The Sun p150, p151; © Dean
Mouhtaropoulos/Getty Images p166 (3); © Dele Alli – Myspace p88
(2); © Ed Garvey/Manchester City FC via Getty Images p89 (11); ©
Eddie Keogh for FA/REX/Shutterstock p77, p91, p103, p117, p139,
p155, p169; © Etsuo Hara/Getty Images p166 (6); © Franck Fife/
AFP/Getty Images p163; © Fred Lee/Getty Images p109, p170–1;
© Fu Tian/China News Service/VCG p87 (top right), p101 (top
right), p101 (top right), p129 (top right), p149 (top right), p165 (top
right), p177 (top right); © Gabriel Bouys/AFP p180; © Ian MacNicol/
Getty Images p43, p56, p63, p176, p182, p24; © Instagram @
harrymaguire93 p88 (3); © Instagram @jesselingard p89 (8); ©
Instagram @jhenderson p89 (10); © Instagram @johnstonesofficial
p89 (7); © Instagram @jpickford1 p88 (4); © Instagram @sterling7
p88 (5); © Instagram @youngy_18 p88 (1); © Jack Taylor/Getty
Images p7; © Jean Catuffe/Getty Images p41, p101 (mid right), p136
(top), p167 (1); © Jewel Samad/AFP/Getty Images p181; © John
Patrick Fletcher/Action Plus via Getty Images p11; © Jon Super for
The FA/REX/Shutterstock p187; © Jonathan Nackstrand/AFP/Getty
Images p137 (top); © Kevin C. Cox/Getty Images p167 (4); © Kyodo
News via Getty Images p167 (6); © Laurence Griffiths/Getty Images
p19, p122–3, p125, p137 (bottom), p185; © Malcolm Croft/PA
Archive/PA Images p186; © Mark Ralston/AFP/Getty Images p166
(5); © Matthew Ashton – AMA/Getty Images p166 (2), p167 (2),
p184; © Matthias Hangst – FIFA/FIFA via Getty Images p26, p31,
p32, p34, p37, p38, p42, p44, p46, p50, p54, p58, p61, p62, p64,
p66, p68, p70, p73; © Matthias Hangst/Getty Images p82, p84–5,
p86, p115 (top), p144; © MB Media/Getty Images p49, p53; ©
Michael Regan – FIFA/FIFA via Getty Images p131; © Mike Hewitt –
FIFA/FIFA via Getty Images p69, p81; © Mladen Antonov/AFP/Getty
Images p118–19, p158; © Nicolas Asfouri/AFP/Getty Images p87
(mid right); © Patrick Hertzog/AFP/Getty Images p104–5; © Pizza
Hut p135; © Quality Sport Images/Getty Images p136 (bottom),
p185, p185, p185; © REX/Shutterstock p89 (9); © Richard Pelham/
The Sun p9, p75; © Robbie Jay Barratt – AMA/Getty Images p142,
p167 (3), p167 (5); © Rolls Press/Popperfoto/Getty Images p13; ©
Sean Gallup/Getty Images p183; © Sebnem Coskun/Anadolu Agency/
Getty Images p182; © Sefa Karacan/Anadolu Agency/Getty Images
p80; © Sergei Savostyanov/TASS via Getty Images p152; © Shaun
Botterill/Getty Images p156–7, p160–1; © Shaun Brooks/Action
Plus via Getty Images p20; © Simon Stacpoole/Offside/Getty Images
p92–3, p126–7; © The Asahi Shimbun via Getty Images p172, p182,
p183; © Tolga Akmen/AFP/Getty Images p129 (bottom), p165
(middle); © Ulrik Pedersen/Action Plus via Getty Images p179; ©
Valery Matytsin/TASS via Getty Images p115 (bottom), p153 (top); ©
VerifiedFollow p89 (6); © VI Images via Getty Images p33, p36, p39;
© Yuri Cortez/AFP/Getty Images p140–1, p146–7; all other images
© Shutterstock.com